Dr Dr, I feel like ... d

Also available from Continuum

Demystifying Postgraduate Research, Jonathon Grix

Research Questions, Richard Andrews

The Research Interview, Bill Gillham

Teaching the Holocaust in School History, Lucy Russell

Dr Dr, I feel like ... doing a PhD

Lucy Russell

continuum

Continuum International Publishing Group

The Tower Building   80 Maiden Lane, Suite 704

11 York Road   New York

SE1 7NX   NY 10038

www.continuumbooks.com

British Library Cataloguing-in-Publication Data

A catalogue record for this book is available from the British Library.

ISBN: 9780826497093 (paperback)

Library of Congress Cataloging-in-Publication Data
Russell, Lucy.
    Dr Dr I feel like– doing a PhD / Lucy Russell.
        p. cm.
    ISBN-13: 978-0-8264-8448-2 (hardcover)
    ISBN-10: 0-8264-8448-4 (hardcover)
    ISBN-13: 978-0-8264-9709-3 (pbk.)
    ISBN-10: 0-8264-9709-8 (pbk.)
    1. Doctor of philosophy degree. 2. Universities and colleges–Graduate work. I. Title.
    LB2386.R87 2008
    378.2'4–dc22

                                        2007045316

Typeset by YHT Ltd, London
Printed and bound in Great Britain by MPG Books, Cornwall

For Jamie
And for Blossom, Sean and Mairéad

Doing a doctorate is a bit like Special Forces selection. The process itself can change you. It is very much about the journey and not about arriving. And, if you are lucky, the journey will continue for the rest of your life.

Victor Newman, Visiting Professor to the Open University Business School in Knowledge Management and Innovation

A PhD can be really intense – mentally and emotionally. And I did go temporarily mad. I can even tell you when it started . . . Now the upside is that it is a properly life-changing, even life-defining experience. You come out of it a sharper and more rounded person.

Dr Michael Corbett

If my PhD did not lead to the sort of career I had been hoping for at the start, it certainly repaid me in other ways. I acquired a confidence that even seemingly impossible problems can be, if not necessarily solved, at least better understood. I discovered that there is real excitement in working on the frontiers of knowledge, and a pleasure in the thought that you may, for a while at least, be the only person who understands a thing, however small that thing may be . . . My PhD was the hardest thing I have ever done; the most consuming; the most threatening to my mental health; and the one I am most proud of . . . It 'empowered' me.

Dr David Kyte

For years while I was bringing up my children I was so depressed. Whenever the children were asleep as babies, or when they were a bit older and were at school, I would be doing things like washing the dishes and making the beds. I felt so fed-up and lonely in the evenings. I would be on my own watching the television while my husband was in another room doing paperwork. Now I am doing my PhD it is like I have a friend. Someone who is always there for me. I'm not bored or lonely any more. I wish I'd done it years ago. I didn't think you could do anything else if you were a mum with small children.

Hattie, second-year PhD student

Contents

Acknowledgements

Thank you to Clyde Chitty and to the PhD students at Goldsmiths College who have attended the Department for Educational Studies' Saturday Schools in the past six years. This book was born out of the Saturday School sessions I have taught with Clyde.

I am grateful to all those who contacted me with their PhD stories. And I am especially grateful to Professor David Bellamy, Professor Clyde Chitty, Professor Hugh Cunningham, Professor Victor Newman and Rabbi Dr Jonathan Romain, for sharing their thoughts and for their commentary.

Special thanks to my cousin, Martha, for the cartoons. Thanks also to Glyn, and to Mum and Dad. I couldn't have done it without you.

Thank you all.

Introduction

Slouching in my pyjamas, I watched as a man on the television discussed the lack of spontaneity in his love life. Meanwhile, commuters filed past my front room window on their way to the train station. Reaching for the remote control, I switched off *Trisha*. Time to do some work.

Becoming a student again takes some getting used to. As a secondary school teacher I looked forward to taking a career break. My time would be my own. There would be no bell every 50 minutes to tell me it was time to start doing something new. I could eat lunch whenever I got hungry, and spend the whole day reading and writing if I wanted to. But at first the lack of routine was disorientating. At times, it was really hard to get motivated. I felt guilty that I had the time to read and think, and do the things *I* wanted to do.

I'd been warned that doing a research degree was a lonely occupation, but I hadn't realized what that meant. Spending several days writing is not so much 'lonely' as maddening. *Trisha* could do a whole programme about it:

'So, when did you first start talking to the toaster?'

'When conversations with myself became predictable.'

Some days I would go out to the supermarket just for an excuse to get showered and dressed. When my partner got in from work, it sometimes took me a few minutes to be able to string a sentence together. Then I would realize I hadn't spoken to anyone all day. I should have given *Trisha* a call. Some 'after-show counselling' would have come in handy to deal with my crippling self-doubt: 'I've chosen completely the wrong topic. Teachers won't read it. They'll be too busy. My thesis is about teaching history, but it won't make any difference to what goes on in schools. It's a waste of time. *What's the point of* ... *anything?*'

Writing a PhD full-time made me question everything, including the meaning of life.

Completing a research degree can be a lonely occupation: many students work alone for much of the time. You think you lack shared experience. You don't get to chat to colleagues over coffee in the staff room. There is no one around to bounce ideas off, or to gain reassurance from. So, realizing that I wasn't alone, and meeting up regularly with others who were also writing at home, was important.

Although I looked forward to the freedom of working from home, I soon discovered there were dangers – like getting sucked into the daytime TV trap. I once saw an interview with Philip Pullman in which he explained that he wrote one thousand words a day, taking a break for the lunchtime edition of *Neighbours*. My problem was that if I didn't switch off immediately after those 20 minutes of light relief, it was impossible to switch off *Diagnosis Murder* without finding out who had killed the football player in the opening scenes ... and so before I knew it, it was time for *Tweenies*.

I found it hard to structure my day. If I worked all day without leaving my flat, I couldn't get to sleep at night. Then I couldn't get up in the morning. Which meant I started work late – then felt guilty about wasting more time. I felt better when I resolved to be up and working by 9am. I tried eight at first, but there was always laundry to put in the washing machine, dishes to wash, the living room to tidy ... Because I was working from home and didn't have to get into work for a certain time, instead of abandoning it all and heading for the door, I felt I had to do these things before I got started.

I also made sure I got showered and dressed. Marian Keyes might be able to write *Under the Duvet* (Keyes, 2001), but I felt better if I was wearing clothes. In the early afternoon I always went for a walk, a swim, or to the gym. Exercise helped me to reflect on what I had done, and plan what I was going to do next. At first I felt guilty that my family and friends were out at work while I was at home, but I told myself this was an opportunity I didn't want to waste. I had flexible working hours! But I wouldn't have them for ever, so why not use the gym when it suited me? If I went in the afternoon, it was quieter.

Over the next nine chapters this book explores 'doing a PhD', and the challenges and rewards of completing this journey. There is no one way to successfully complete a doctorate, but there are a number of wrong ways – like having your ego flattered into it, or because you can't think of what else you would like to do. I really wanted to do a PhD, but there were times when I hated it. If you are less than convinced that you want to do a PhD at the start, it makes it less likely that you will finish it.

This book is about what it's like to submit yourself to the process of doing a doctorate. It's about how it *feels* to be a research student: the elation, the guilt, the isolation, the self-doubt, the loneliness. In describing this a number of practical issues are discussed: choosing a topic, finding funding, writing a proposal, methods of research, the literature review, academic writing, the question of 'truth' in research, the relationship between student and supervisor, maintaining your focus, and preparing for a viva examination. As well as reflecting on my own experience, the following chapters reflect on the experience of others. While writing this book it has become very clear that students' experience of the PhD process is very similar irrespective of who they are or when they completed their PhD.

Doing a doctorate changes you as a person. It is not simply about acquiring subject knowledge. It changes the way you think, and how you understand the world around you. Once my initial feelings of guilt and isolation subsided, I felt liberated. It was hard to make the break and leave my job, but after just one term I remembered why I'd decided to go into teaching in the first place! Already I had ideas about what I would do differently when I went back into the classroom.

It was amazing to have the time and space and to exercise the mind, and exorcise familiar worries about (unnecessary) paperwork, parents' evenings and pensions – just for a few years – and do something *I* really wanted to, rather than things my ego had been flattered into accepting. It was a reminder of the importance of education for its own sake.

Writing a PhD was something I had always wanted to do. When I achieved that opportunity, it took some time for me to readjust. Grasp your opportunity and make the most of it; and use any spare time to do things you have wanted to do in the past but haven't had the time to ... the '50 minute bell' will return.

Chapter One

Can you write a prescription?

'Excuse my ignorance, but what's a PhD?'

That's a question I've been asked many times. On this occasion it came from a bank clerk while I was opening a new account. When I left my teaching job to do a PhD, it was a question my pupils wanted an answer to:

'Why are you leaving?' asked Liam.

'I'm going back to university to do another degree. I'm going to do some research about teaching history. When I've finished, I'll be called Dr Russell.'

'Will you be able to write prescriptions?'

'No, it's a title that means you've done a certain amount of study.'

Smiling at me, Liam replied, 'So, you'll be like a doctor of dates. When someone forgets when the Battle of Hastings was, they'll come to your surgery and you'll tell them, "1066".'

What is a PhD?

In a nutshell, that is what a PhD is: a degree higher than an Honours or Masters degree, which is gained by completing at least two and a half years of supervised research. The major task for the PhD student is the writing up of their research (which should make an original contribution to existing knowledge – there is more on this in Chapter Two) in the form of a 50,000- to 100,000-word thesis (depending on the requirements of their academic department).

The word 'thesis' is Greek in origin, and means 'position'. After the thesis is submitted there is an oral examination (the viva – short for *viva voce* which is Latin for 'with the living voice' or 'by word of mouth'), where the student must defend their 'position'. Someone with a PhD (these letters are an abbreviation of the Latin *Philosophiæ Doctor* or *Doctor Philosophiæ*) is entitled to call themselves 'Doctor'.

How long does it take?
It usually takes between three and six years to complete a PhD, depending on whether you are a full-time or part-time student. There are minimum and maximum periods of registration (this is the time it takes from registering with a university and starting your research to submitting your thesis). It depends on the institution, but usually you have to be enrolled on a PhD programme for at least two years if you are a full-time student, and four years if you are part-time. The maximum period of

enrolment on a PhD programme is generally four years full-time and six years part-time. I have never heard of anybody who has completed their PhD in two years. Three years is still seen as pretty fast work. If you are stuggling to finish your PhD full-time within the maximum amount of time allowed, you can ask to transfer to part-time status. If something comes up and gets in the way of your progress, like a new job, a bereavement, or some other personal difficulty, then whether you are a full-time or part-time student you can also ask your head of programme for a 'formal interruption' – that means putting your study on hold.

How do you organize a thesis?

Typically a thesis consists of a comprehensive 'literature review', an outline of a methodology, and several chapters of scientific, social, historical, philosophical or literary analysis. The term 'literature review' can be confusing – it doesn't mean listing and summarizing all the books you've read. You don't actually have to dedicate a chapter to a literature review; history theses don't usually have one. My thesis was in education, and I didn't write a literature review as such. What the literature review *must* do is show that you know about the recent developments, challenges and debates in your chosen field. I wrote a chapter entitled 'Issues Surrounding Teaching the Holocaust in School History' in which I highlighted and debated the key issues, drawing on the literature I had read. Other forms of media like radio and television programmes, as well as newspapers, also count as 'literature'.

If you are thinking about a framework for your PhD, it will probably start with an introductory chapter in which you 'position yourself' in the research. This would be a piece of writing which says 'this is me and this is where I am coming from' (there is more on this in Chapter Five). Having located yourself, you need to locate your research in your field of study. So you would write a chapter showing that you have read around your subject, addressing questions like: What has already been done in this area? What is the current thinking on the topic? What has gone before? (Thereby also demonstrating that what you are doing is new, i.e. *original*.)

Then you write your 'methodology' chapter, in which you

would set out what you are trying to find out and how you intend to do this (what methods are you going to use?). You need to show an awareness of philosophy in this chapter, and the theories underpinning the methods you have chosen to use.

Next, you have a couple of chapters presenting what you have found out, before writing a concluding chapter in which you interpret and reflect on your findings − and perhaps identify areas for future research. The whole thesis should build towards this final chapter, and as with any conclusion it shouldn't present anything new to the reader.

That − in essence − is what a PhD is. But ...

Why would you want a PhD?

Rabbi Dr Jonathan Romain is a writer and broadcaster. He serves as minister of the Maidenhead Synagogue in Berkshire. He decided to complete a PhD because,

> having just been ordained as a rabbi, I was about to enter congregational life, to which I was looking forward, but I knew it would be all too easy to get totally immersed in the everyday duties of 'hatch, match and dispatch' and I also wanted to keep my academic interests alive − so doing a PhD was a good way of achieving this. To be honest, there was also a bit of me that thought: wouldn't it be nice not only to be 'Rabbi Romain' but 'Rabbi Dr Romain' − it sounds so much better! − although that by itself wouldn't have been enough to justify all the hard work involved.

There was part of me which was motivated by the desire to become 'Dr Russell'. If I'm honest, I think failing my 11-plus, and doing less well than I and my teachers expected at A level, left me feeling I had something to prove. Professor David Bellamy completed his PhD in Mire Ecology at Bedford College, London (now part of Royal Holloway). He wanted to do a PhD because it is 'the highest accolade of academia'. Dr Christine Wall said she wanted to challenge herself and 'see how far I could get academically ... I liked the idea of having a whole piece of new research of my own, having spent many years researching as part of a team'. For others, like Dr Charles

Campbell, it was more a case of not knowing the next step in his chosen career:

> As a final-year undergraduate, I was far more focused on the looming threat of finals than in making arrangements for my future career – I suppose I had always assumed that if I attained the best possible degree, everything else would simply fall into place. Friends and peers would spend hours in the careers office poring over company brochures and con-structing perfect application letters, though all, it seemed, to little avail. During my degree I had been fortunate to take a one-year placement in a biotech company and this had given me what I thought was a useful insight into the industry: everybody in the upper echelons of that company had done their time and had the initials PhD (or DPhil) after their name. It struck me then that the qualification served as some sort of rite of passage into the scientific community which, in a sense, I suppose it is. As such, embarking on a PhD struck me as the next logical career step, as well as a reasonable (and convenient) way of filling that postgraduate vacuum. But as the viva lists were posted on our departmental board I still had no clear plan mapped out. It was perhaps fortunate then that I was called for a viva.
>
> The viva was not a particularly gruelling or challenging examination. In fact it was immediately impressed on me that I could consider it a routine procedure. The professor and I spent more time discussing my future, and I ended up leaving the room with a tentative offer of a PhD studentship. More importantly, it was one of the best-funded studentships available at the time, and in a highly regarded lab at one of the UK's leading universities. The research project sounded interesting enough and so I agreed to attend an informal interview. I confess that my career was at the forefront of my mind, rather than the noble calling of academic pursuit for the sake of academic pursuit – a situation which I believe was generally mirrored by others in my peer group who headed off to their own respective PhD laboratories.

Professor Hugh Cunningham (well known for his books and

his 30-part series for BBC Radio 4 in 2006, *The Invention of Childhood*) decided to do a PhD because he wanted an academic career. Your own reasons for doing a PhD will obviously be more worthy than a desire to collect anecdotes which you can dine out on. But this is a by-product, and Hugh tells a story about photocopying in the House of Lords record office:

> I wanted to photocopy quite a lot of the printed petitions to the House of Commons which were held in the House of Lords Records Office. It was agreed I could do this, but there either wasn't a photocopier in the Records Office or it wasn't available, so arrangements were made for me to do the photocopying in some back room of the House of Commons, provided I did it after midnight. At about 2am my enthusiasm for photocopying was too much for the machine, which began to smoke alarmingly. Mindful of precedents, I turned it off and made a run for it.

I think I'd have done the same. I did visit the Houses of Parliament during my own research. The House of Lords actually appeared on one of my bank statements as the location of a cash machine withdrawal! I had gone to look through Hansard, to find a reference to a House of Lords debate about teaching materials on the topic of the Holocaust produced by the Inner London Education Authority in the 1980s. Eventually, I found the debate and asked if I could have a copy of it. There was no facility to do your own photocopying (since when, I wonder? ...). I had some cash, but not enough to cover the cost (it was going to be nearly £20 for all the pages I wanted), and there was no way of getting any money inside the Palaces of Westminster. Unless, that is, I could sweet-talk a porter into walking me to the Lords' cash point ... Now, 'Baroness Dr Russell' would be quite a title wouldn't it?

I learned what a PhD was, and decided I liked the idea of doing one, while watching *Inspector Morse* in my mid-teens. Academic life, minus the murders, seemed attractive. I did not go to Oxbridge. I went to the University of Kent at Canterbury. My undergraduate dissertation (which looked at the effects of the 1984–5 miners' strike on my local community) was well received. A sociology lecturer, who was working at

Kent as a visiting tutor while completing his own PhD, looked over my dissertation and said, 'You should do a PhD.'

'Don't I need to do an MA first?'

'No. You could go straight to PhD. You need to get hold of a book called ...' I bought a copy of the book. I even read some of it, but not much. It was a bit dry. Maybe I would think about a higher degree in a few years, after I'd gained a professional qualification and worked for a bit. On my graduation day the Economic and Social History Department had a party. One of my tutors came over to talk to me: 'You know, I was impressed with your dissertation. I think you could get it published ...' The seeds were sown.

However, by then I had a place on a PGCE (Postgraduate Certificate in Education) course at Canterbury Christ Church University College to become a teacher. I didn't know anything about studentships and funding, and it didn't occur to me to find out about staying at Kent to pursue an academic career. Anyway, I didn't think I could afford to do it (see Chapter Three for ideas on funding).

Coming up with a research question

At the end of my PGCE year I abridged my undergraduate dissertation and sent it to various publications. Eventually it was published in *The Historian* in the Winter 1999 edition. I wanted to write more. In January 2000 I gave a talk to PGCE students at Canterbury Christ Church University College about being a Newly Qualified Teacher. Later, in the pub, my mentor suggested I rewrite it and see if *Teaching History* would publish it. I did, and they did. I was enjoying teaching – but I loved writing. I started thinking again about doing a PhD. Maybe I could do both, part-time. I needed a research question. What was I interested in?

It was 2000, and the furore about the Millennium Dome never seemed to be out of the headlines. According to the advertising, a visit to the Dome was supposed to be 'One amazing day'. But the press was full of stories about poor ticket sales, with the Government repeatedly having to bail out the project with more money from public funds. I thought about the success of the 1851 Great Exhibition. Why had the Dome failed? I rang a professor, an old tutor, at Kent University. Did he think this could be a PhD question? He thought it had potential. I visited the Dome. I started to do some reading. But there was too much schoolwork to do. I ended up turning my initial research into another article for *The Historian*.

If you are struggling to find a research question, think about topics you might be interested in. What aspects are interesting? Are any unexplored? It might be worth reading PhD theses in the area you are interested in, to see if there are any questions for future research, or if throwaway suggestions might provide you with some inspiration. Reading other theses will also give you an idea of the academic standard expected. But don't be intimidated – I used to read other theses and think, 'I'll never be able to write like this!' Now, if I pick up my own thesis or read the book I wrote based on it, I think, 'I can't believe *I* wrote this!'

Towards the end of my second year of teaching, I was looking through the Appointments section in the *Guardian*. Goldsmiths College was advertising PhD studentships in Education. Three years, fully funded. I sent for the details and an application form. I needed an idea. I thought about my lessons, and what I had been teaching that term: I had been struggling to teach about the Holocaust.

The Holocaust forces us to confront the limits of human behaviour. As I stood in front of a class of 13 and 14 year olds teaching about the Nuremberg Laws, I had wondered what exactly I was trying to achieve. It was a difficult lesson. Pupils had not grasped what it meant to be Jewish. I was fielding questions like 'Why didn't the Jews convert to another religion? Couldn't they wear coloured contact lenses, or dye their hair, to escape from the Nazis?' What did I want my pupils to leave the classroom with? An understanding of the Nuremberg laws? Empathy with the Jews? A realization that racism and prejudice is wrong? Some knowledge of the context for the Second World War? I wondered how the Holocaust was taught in other countries, including Germany. I recalled a college lecturer talking about the National Curriculum review which took place while I was at teaching college in 1999. At one point during the drafting of the revised history curriculum, the

Holocaust was apparently the only specified compulsory content (Haydn, 2000, p. 135). The topic of the Holocaust – perhaps because it is such a human event – prompted me to reflect on the role of history in the school curriculum. There seemed to be mileage here for a PhD study. I wanted to find out why the Holocaust was considered such a fundamental part of the history curriculum, and what impact that had on how it was conceptualized and taught as a school subject.

I was offered a studentship at Goldsmiths to complete my research. I had an Honours degree (2:1) in Economic and Social History and Sociology; I did not have a Masters degree. Quite often a good 2:1 and a solid research proposal is all you need. I found out later that it helped my application to have had work published.

Do you really want a PhD? Why?

Research goes in cycles: there is excitement and exhilaration, as well as disenchantment and despair. It is best to start out excited and interested in what you are proposing to do. A minimum of three years is a long time to be working on one topic. So whatever you decide to study, to keep you motivated it must be a topic that you enjoy and have a genuine interest in. Even then, it is likely that you will, at times, become bored with what you are doing, or even overwhelmed by a sense of pointlessness.

There were three reasons I wanted to do a PhD: for myself; for its own sake; and because I wanted to find out more about the curriculum I was teaching. I think there is much to be said for pursuing an education for its own sake, though this is not a view shared by Charles Clarke, who commented in 2003 (when he was Secretary of State for Education) that this idea was 'a bit dodgy'. The *Times Higher Education Supplement* reported on 9 May that year that:

> Education secretary Charles Clarke has again attacked learning for learning's sake by saying that the public purse should not fund 'ornamental' subjects such as medieval history. Mr Clarke told a gathering at University College, Worcester, that he believed the state should pay only for

higher education that had a 'clear usefulness'. He reportedly said: 'I don't mind there being some medievalists around for ornamental purposes, but there is no reason for the state to pay for them.' This follows his earlier comments that studying classics is a waste of time.

(Baty, 2003)

Clarke's definition of education seems rather narrow. Education is surely about more than 'usefulness'. I believe it is about learning to think. The PhD experience isn't always what those embarking upon it expect it to be; and it doesn't always take them to where they think they will end up. It goes beyond usefulness. Look at the comments of those I have quoted at the start of this book. Victor stresses the importance of the journey – the PhD process; Michael reflects that a PhD is a life-changing experience; and David talks about empowerment. Christine Wall embarked on her PhD aged 40: it was something she was doing for herself, not to further her career:

> Did I enjoy doing the PhD? I certainly did. I enjoyed the challenge. I found I could cope with the down times when none of the experiments worked (this is the time when some younger PhD students give up). I enjoyed presenting my work at scientific meetings; attending these meetings was so much more relevant when you were doing your own original work. I enjoyed working with outside collaborators, all of whom expanded my scientific horizons.

Queen guitarist Dr Brian May (also a former teacher; he taught maths at a comprehensive school at the same time as doing his PhD research, before he decided to focus solely on his music) completed and submitted his PhD 33 years after abandoning it to join Queen. Brian is an inspiration for those who harbour a desire to complete a doctorate: aged 60, and with an already hugely successful career, his motivation was a love for his subject. He told the BBC, 'Astronomy has always interested me' (BBC News, 3 August 2007).

But for some, completing a PhD *is* about usefulness in the sense that it is the beginning of their academic career. A doctorate was originally a licence to practise as a teacher in a university. The word 'doctor' is derived from the Latin for 'teacher' (not 'healer' – see Chapter Four). Today, competition for academic posts is so intense that a PhD is necessary. It is a professional qualification which says, 'I can design and complete research to a standard which is worthy of a university post.' Having a PhD is also seen as signifying that someone is an authority on a subject, and that they have made a contribution to the current knowledge in that area.

Outside academia, employers may be impressed by candidates who have a doctorate, but they are more likely to place value on the skills gained through completing a PhD, like self-motivation, and research and analytical skills – rather than being impressed by the doctorate itself, or the subject knowledge acquired in the process.

There is debate within the academy about what a PhD is for. Clyde Chitty is Professor of Policy and Management in Education at Goldsmiths College. He thinks you do PhD research to try and change the world: 'I do believe that a PhD should have a social and/or political purpose. I wonder if it is worthwhile, if it is allowed to gather dust on the shelves.' But not all academics agree. Others believe you do doctoral research to get a PhD and an academic post; and that it doesn't much matter whether other people read your work. Research does not *have* to be useful. Professor Carrie Paechter, also of Goldsmiths College, has written on goodness and utility in educational research:

> In recent years – and probably for much longer – there have been repeated pronouncements by governments, policy makers and others that focused on the utility, or lack of it, of educational research. These pronouncements appear mainly to have concentrated on complaints that educational researchers are ivory-tower academics who do little that has any relation to the real world and, in any case, if they do, fail to disseminate it properly to 'end users', the (often undefined) people who need it.
>
> (Paechter, 2003, p. 105)

But, argues Paechter:

> My (possibly radical) proposal is that, as educational researchers, we should focus on conducting good research in

the field of education and trust to its utility. We are not always able to predict which areas will be most fertile for investigation, nor which studies will have most long-term impact. However, I think that anything that tells us more about the world of education (very broadly conceived) will be useful at some point. As long as we ensure that we carry out our work as well as it is possible to do so, with due regard to an underpinning moral imperative, rigour, transparency, connection to theory and research ethics, we will be contributing to knowledge in the field of education. This should be our purpose.

(p. 116)

Whether you are interested in completing research which will be immediately useful and has a social or political purpose, or you want to do some research for the sake of it, 'doing a PhD is about deciding to be in control of your thinking process over an extended period of time' (Professor Victor Newman).

To get a PhD, you really need to be convinced about your goal and purpose. Not really wanting it means you probably won't get it. Andrew Marr began a PhD but didn't finish it, possibly because his heart wasn't in it. Writing about his career in his book *My Trade: A Short History of British Journalism*, he says that he

stumbled into journalism. I'd done the requisite English degree, played politics, drawn cartoons and learned how to smoke sixty cigarettes a day without being sick. I'd started a PhD, washed dishes and been turned down for a job in a second-hand bookshop. Despite having a first-class degree and having read an unfeasibly large number of books, it began to dawn on me that I couldn't actually *do* anything.

(Marr, 2004, p. xvi)

After graduating from King's College, Cambridge, with a double first in English literature, comedian David Baddiel went to University College, London, to do a PhD in English, 'though that was really just so I could get the £3,000 a term grant to cover my expenses while I did comedy', he told the *Independent*: 'I did work hard on it, I just didn't get to finish it' (26 January 2006). If your PhD is not your first love, or if you take another job, or pursue other interests while trying to complete your research, then time and attention are inevitably taken away from your study, and if you are distracted or you don't want it enough, it is unlikely you will finish it. I have friends whose PhDs have been scuppered by them accepting a new job before finishing their doctorate. They had less time for their studies, and the job took priority as they tried to make their mark in the workplace. As a result, their PhDs went on the back burner, and stayed there.

Rabbi Dr Jonathan Romain dispenses the following good advice. What is important about PhD research is that:

> you have a passion for your subject, as you are going to live, eat and breathe it for at least two years, maybe more, and you want to be sufficiently in love with your theme to have the will to complete it. Equally essential is the desire to write something that no one else in the world has done before.

If this is *your* desire, read on!

Chapter Two

A penny for your thoughts

'I'm glad your robes are red. It made it much easier to find you.'

It was a beautiful autumn day. I was standing on the lawn behind the college, listening to the jazz band, while I waited for my family. I had 'processed' here from my graduation ceremony in the Great Hall. A friend had commented earlier in the day, 'It's funny. The college is so trendy and cutting-edge till graduation day – then, we're transported back to medieval England.' Modern academic dress – like the graduation ceremony itself – dates back to the twelfth and thirteenth centuries when universities, as we now know them, were developing. Academic gowns are derived from the dress of the medieval clergy. The church had a monopoly on education, partly because the church was the guardian of 'true' doctrine, and partly because in the main only the clergy could read and write. Designed for warmth in unheated buildings (as opposed to an autumn day with temperatures in the high 20s!) robes were closed down the front, like a cassock. When Oxford and Cambridge first began prescribing academic dress during the reign of Henry VIII the robes were opened up, in line with English fashion at the time, to reveal rich lining and fine clothes beneath.

The sun was beating down, so I didn't keep my Tudor bonnet on (a hat with a stiff oval brim and a soft velvet top in plain black) for very long. Again, this headgear was the height of fashion in Henry's day. Although it might not be fashionable these days, I enjoyed being part of the history and tradition. It was a wonderful day, which rounded off three years of hard work.

There is no single way to make it to graduation day and no single way to do a PhD. The course of the research is completely determined by the researcher: there is no syllabus, no set reading list. Although you will be assigned a supervisor to work with, ultimately you decide how you are going to complete your research. You set your own deadlines. At the viva you will have to defend the decisions you made about how you conducted your research. There are no universal, precise criteria for a successful PhD, there is no clear 'gold standard'. It is more of a question of whether your thesis has the 'x-factor'. Much depends on the interpretation and evaluation of 'originality' and 'contribution to knowledge' and whether the thesis 'reaches a publishable standard in its whole or in part'. The requirement to make an original contribution to existing knowledge in your chosen field of study sounds scarier than it is. You can demonstrate originality by discovering and presenting new facts in your thesis, or cast new light on existing knowledge by using your independent critical power.

Finding funding

There is not enough money to support all the research that could be done, and for those who are thinking about embarking on a research degree, the deciding factor is often funding. This is one of the first things you will need to consider and organize. Many university departments offer annual studentships – also known as scholarships or bursaries. In addition to having their fees paid students receive an annual stipend, paid monthly, of around £10–12,000. This is tax-free. These awards often require the student to do some teaching within the department (this is a good thing to do – there is more on this in Chapter Three). If you are interested in doing a PhD at a particular university, check with the relevant department whether they offer studentships, or whether they can give you any advice about funding. A useful website, which provides a comprehensive guide to PhD studentships and postgraduate degrees, is www.findaphd.com. Studentships usually begin at the start of the academic year and run for three years. The deadline for applications is generally around May or June. But there are often other awards available too, in specific fields at particular institutions – perhaps sponsored by individual donors, or public or private organizations. These research programmes could start any time, and you can apply to enrol on a post-graduate research degree – and begin it – at any point in the academic year.

Some funding also comes from the government. There are seven Research Councils in the United Kingdom which distribute government funding across various subject areas. These are the Arts and Humanities Research Council; Biotechnology and Biological Sciences Research Council; Engineering and Physical Sciences Research Council; Economic and Social Research Council; Medical Research Council; Natural Environment Research Council; and the Science and Technology Facilities Council. As a postgraduate you can only apply directly to the Arts and Humanities Research Council for funding. There are certain residency and academic criteria, but you can check whether you are eligible to apply for a doctoral award (the Council offers full awards which cover fees and a maintenance grant, and fees-only awards) on the Arts and Humanities Research Council website, www.ahrb.ac.uk. The Economic and Social Research Council also has a funding guide on its website, www.esrcsocietytoday.ac.uk. Their research grants provide support for specific research projects in the social sciences, but you need to apply with your supervisor for one of these grants. Similarly you can apply, with the support of your institution, to the Science and Technologies Research Council for a grant to complete your research. Details are available at www.stfc.ac.uk.

The other research councils don't give money to students directly; they distribute money under various schemes to institutions, and places on the programmes they help to fund are advertised by the institution involved. In these cases you are applying for already-prepared topics, and you won't need to write a proposal. Check the education press for details. It is also worth talking to your bank about a graduate or career development loan.

The proposal

A research proposal and a proposal of marriage are not dis-similar. Both signify a serious commitment; neither is to be entered into lightly. When you sit down to write a research proposal, there are three key questions to think about: What are you proposing to write about? How do you propose to complete your project? And why is the research important – how do you think it will make an original contribution to knowledge in your subject area? When thinking about this third question, consider how you can make your proposed topic look attractive to the university department you are applying to. Also, think about how the topic can be developed in the future, beyond your PhD. The emphasis really is on the word 'proposal' – exactly what your PhD research is about, and how it is conducted, cannot be set in stone until later.

Having outlined what you want to find out about, you need to think about how you plan to find out what you want to know! What methods do you think you would use? It doesn't matter if your ideas change once you have begun your PhD. I had various ideas about observing history teachers teaching a lesson on the Holocaust; talking to students in focus groups about their experience of history lessons on this topic; interviewing teachers who took their classes to the Holocaust Exhibition at the Imperial War Museum ... My original proposal involved comparing the teaching of the Holocaust in German and English schools. But I couldn't speak German, and after discussing my proposal with a former tutor at Christ Church I realized this would not work out. The deadline for applications to Goldsmiths had passed a day or two before, but I decided to re-submit an amended proposal. I had nothing to lose! I faxed a letter and my new proposal to the head of the PhD programme, and hoped for the best.

My first question at interview was: 'Why has your proposal changed?' I answered honestly. I think this showed that I had given my proposal serious thought. It was a good interview – I enjoyed talking about my ideas and the writing I had done – but it was also the toughest interview I've ever had. There were seven academics sitting in a horseshoe in front of me, all asking questions. I sat at the bottom of the horseshoe – by the door. What is funny is that I never even thought about bolting through that door. I felt more confident and in control at that point than when I had been awarded the studentship – which should have given me greater confidence. I didn't doubt my ability for a second, until I actually began my research. At that point, I wondered whether I really was worthy of the academy. During that first term I had to keep telling myself that I was worthy, and that those seven academics must have had faith in me.

My proposal set out the aims and objectives of my research; the methodology and proposed structure of my thesis; and a list of relevant reading. This proposal included my intention to observe history teachers teaching about the Holocaust, and to interview them; I designed pro formas for this purpose and included them in my proposal, which began with a statement about the aim of my research:

> The National Curriculum for History in England demands only that the Holocaust, the two World Wars and the Cold War are taught, advising of various other characters and periods of history which could be taught. Unlike elsewhere in Europe where the National Curriculum is compulsory to the age of 16, in England it is optional at age 14. As a result the Holocaust is usually taught in Year 9 (to 13- and 14-year-old pupils). The Holocaust as a topic presents challenges to history teachers, which seem to stem from confusion over objectives. At a recent seminar on approaches to teaching the Holocaust, at the Imperial War Museum in London, it was clear that the perceived aims of teaching the Holocaust in history varied, as did the number of history lessons spent on the topic. The teachers present also admitted being more emotional in their delivery of Holocaust education than in teaching any other period or event in history. They felt a great sense of responsibility in teaching the subject, and thought it was important to 'get it right'. My study seeks to explore the different strategies employed by history teachers in delivering the Holocaust within the history curriculum.

It may be useful to refer to your research proposal once you have begun your research, in order to help you maintain a clear focus. But quite often, the research proposed and the research completed are different. As I started to explore the history of the Holocaust as a topic in the National Curriculum for History, my research shifted slightly to look, firstly, at why the topic of the Holocaust had become compulsory when it was not recommended in the draft proposals about what should be in the new National Curriculum; and secondly, what impact making the topic compulsory had had on history teachers and their teaching.

There are different types of research, monitored by the Research Assessment Exercise (RAE), which is carried out every four to five years by a panel of academics who judge the output of academic research from every higher education institution and, having considered the results, decide how funding should be distributed among universities; there is more on the RAE at www.rae.ac.uk. In 2001 the Higher Education Research Council classified research into three areas: *basic research*, where an original contribution to knowledge or the development of a theory is made (my work would have fallen into this bracket); *strategic research*, which tests the generalizations and theories which emerge from basic research to see whether broader generalizations can be made – if such and such is true of *x*, it may also be true of *y*; and *applied research*, where you are carrying out work with a specific practical objective in mind – you are looking for a solution to a problem.

Don't get too hung up on these categories, Judith Bell writes at the beginning of her book, *Doing Your Research Project*: 'It is perfectly possible to carry out a worthwhile investigation without having detailed knowledge of the various approaches to or styles of educational research.' But she goes on to say that 'a study of different approaches will give insight into different ways of planning an investigation, and, incidentally, will also enhance your understanding of the literature' (Bell, 1999, p. 7). The methods you choose to use will be determined by the field in which you are working, and what you want to find out. There are a number of texts to guide you. I found *Research Methods in Education* helpful (Cohen, Manion and Morrison, 2003). The books of Cohen et al. and Judith Bell both have 'education' in the title, but would also be very useful to those completing research in other fields.

It's all good fun. Isn't it?

Once funding is sorted out and you have a university place to complete your doctorate, you will probably feel like cracking open the champagne. And quite right. But you may be getting the idea by now that it is a long road, and the journey is 'profoundly disorientating' (Victor Newman). Don't expect the process to be fun. Do expect it to take over your life. Feelings of guilt and isolation, as described in the introduction, are not uncommon among research students. Clyde Chitty explains:

> To begin with, I found the experience lonely and daunting. I was just 40 years old and I had been principal of a Leicestershire community college, surrounded by people all the time. All of a sudden, I was on my own, feeling guilty about *not* working. So I was really happy when the Institute of Education offered me a lecturer's post in the Curriculum Studies Department. Once again I felt 'needed' and 'socially useful'. Also, I could discuss my ideas and findings with colleagues and students, and I welcomed their insights and criticism. I no longer felt guilty about being at home, while other people were at work.

This sense of loneliness and isolation is not experienced by all PhD students. Dr Mark Tuckett, as a PhD student, had a very different experience. Science- and engineering-based PhDs that involve lab work can foster great camaraderie. But that isn't always the case. After taking up his studentship and being introduced to his department, Dr Charles Campbell was 'guided away from the communal lab to a small windowless room in which I was obliged to conduct my research ... Days would go by without my speaking to anybody at work, trapped as I was in my solitary confinement'.

Charles hadn't anticipated that his PhD would have the impact upon him that it did:

> My studentship began in what can probably be considered a fairly routine manner. I was introduced to the department and attended a meeting with other new students where we were introduced to the Dean. He informed the packed room that somewhere between 18 months and 2 years into our

research we would each face an uphill struggle. There would be no light at the end of the tunnel, and we would see no way out. We would despair! Everybody did, and we were to rest assured that this was all quite normal. 'Not I!' I remember thinking. I was still flushed with the success of my degree. I would succeed without even struggling. I returned to my department, still confident.

My first task was to design an experimental model. I met with my supervisor on an ad hoc basis, but since she had never actually designed a comparable model herself, there wasn't much technical support she could realistically give. The practical work was completely new to me, and in retrospect I received woefully inadequate instruction and was obliged to teach myself many of the intricate techniques. I struggled on and twelve months later I still could not get anything to work in a reproducible manner – twelve months out of a total of thirty-six were gone, and I didn't have a single piece of hard data. Suddenly, things were not looking so rosy. It wasn't just that I had the prospect of a thesis without results to consider. No results meant no research papers. No papers, no future research grant. No research grant, no research. No research, no career. No career, no income. I began to feel increasingly helpless. Anxiety gradually became an ever-present feature in my life. The biggest problem was that I had no real way to overcome that destructive emotion. In the past, if the cause had been exams, an essay deadline, or something trivial such as no money for beer, a solution could be engineered and the anxiety controlled: study harder, sacrifice a weekend to the essay or secure another loan. But now it seemed there was nothing I could do. I spoke with my supervisor and she advised me to keep plugging away in the lab. But no matter what I did, nothing changed. It just didn't bloody work!

I became superstitious. I used to cycle to the university, and if I didn't get held up at a red traffic light my luck would be in and the experiment would reproduce that day. But nature chose not to adhere to my ridiculous rules. I would make a miniscule error, or infernal variability would produce an outlying result. Again I called on my supervisor and she gave me one piece of advice which, though arguably useful for everyday life, didn't really help me much at the time: everybody makes mistakes; the trick is to only make them once.

But Charles's predicament got even worse:

Things began to spiral out of control and I began to find it increasingly difficult to maintain perspective. I took out my frustrations on the squash court or the running track. I just needed more time! I had ideas! Hypotheses I could prove, or otherwise, if only I could get my experimental model to work. I knew I was a good scientist, but unlike other students I had nothing to show for it: no *Nature* papers in the offing, no lab book bursting with data, no thesis as good as done, and no lab head clamouring to secure me a post-doctoral position in their group. Such things seemed a pipe dream from my perspective at that time, and further battered my self-esteem.

With no real means of release for my growing concerns I began to feel increasingly melancholic. This put considerable strain on my relationship with my girlfriend. I'd have night sweats and frequently cry in the mornings, sometimes unwilling to resume what I now considered as my futile battle. She would talk me through it each morning and eventually persuade me to get going. I would don a mask of self-assuredness and head off. At night, I would return home, the mask would slip, and she would try to calm me, talking to me to ease the knot in my stomach so that I could sleep. This wasn't me! I had no idea what was happening. All I knew was that I would not, could not, quit. Eventually I was forced to seek professional help.

Things did eventually turn around for Charles. There is more of his story later. His experiences are not uncommon. 'It's no wonder that some people find the responsibility too stressful,' says Professor Victor Newman, 'and that when friends asked me what my thesis was about, I would hesitate comically and my wife would jump in and précis my hypothesis while I nodded helplessly in approximate agreement, my head cocked critically to one side.' Professor David Bellamy described completing his PhD as 'enervating'.

During a speech at Exeter University in July 2007, Dr Brian May is reported to have told students, 'For the last nine months I've done nothing except slave over my PhD, which is now written up, thank God. But there are times when you really want to give up. There are times when you go, "Why on earth did I take this on?"' (Ireland On-Line, 15 July 2007). Rabbi Dr Jonathan Romain agrees that a PhD is 'hard work'. But he did also find the experience 'highly enjoyable'. Like Hattie, who is quoted at the start of this book, he seems to have found the companionship of his PhD a pleasure, though 'the frustration was doing it part-time alongside a full-time job, and having to force myself to snatch time here and there for it – but it did mean that it was a place to which I could retreat that was just for me'. Hattie also has a part-time job in higher education. And Dr Tobias Feakin worked part time to fund his study. He found that this 'proved quite a strain' and 'wouldn't endorse this because it becomes very difficult' in terms of time. Although the lack of time must be frustrating, it seems that having a job resulted, for Jonathan and Hattie, in a more positive relationship between researcher and research. Jonathan and Hattie both regard their research as a pleasure. I had thought that I would too, and in the end I did. But initially I was overwhelmed by guilt and isolation.

'You don't understand ...'
The PhD experience can impact upon your life in other ways you don't expect. I was surprised when one student asked me how my partner felt about me doing a PhD, and whether it had had an impact on our relationship: it wasn't something I had thought about. To onlookers, doing a research degree full-time can look like a charmed life – and in one sense it is; but there are challenges. Some students complain that their partners don't understand what they are doing, or the pressure they are under. There are those who don't understand why anyone would want to do a higher degree. I remember one of my religious education teachers commenting that it might sound ridiculous to us

but it was important to marry someone who was our intellectual equal. She was right! Aged 14 I did think this comment
sounded ridiculous, but I now see her point. In Willy Russell's
play *Educating Rita*, 'Rita's' husband (her real name is Susan, but
she has changed her name because *Rubyfruit Jungle* by Rita Mae
Brown is her favourite book) Denny simply cannot understand
why she wants to do an Open University course rather than
accept her lot and have a baby with him. In the opening scene
of the play Rita explains why she wanted to complete an Open
University course:

> Rita: I've been realizin' for ages that I was, y'know, slightly
> out of step. I'm twenty-six. I should have had a baby by now;
> everyone expects it. I'm sure me husband thinks I'm sterile.
> He was moanin' all the time, y'know, 'Come off the pill, let's
> have a baby.' I told him I'd come off it, just to shut him up.
> But I'm still on it. See, I don't want a baby yet. See, I wanna
> discover meself first. Do you understand that?

> Frank: Yes.

> Rita: Yeh. They wouldn't round our way. They'd think I
> was mental. I've tried to explain to me husband but between
> you an' me I think he's thick. No, he's not thick, he's blind,
> he doesn't want to see. You know if I'm readin', or watchin'
> somethin' different on the telly he gets dead narked. I used to
> just tell him to piss off but then I realized it was no good
> doin' that, that I had to explain to him. I tried to explain that
> I wanted a better way of livin' me life. An' he listened to me.
> But he didn't understand because when I had finished he said
> he agreed with me and that we should start savin' the money
> to move off our estate an' get a house out in Formby ...
>   (W. Russell, 1986, pp. 178–9)

Students sometimes talk about the fact that their partner's
families don't understand why they are doing a PhD rather than
a 'real' job. They see their own son or daughter out working
and perceive their partner as an 'eternal student' who is living
off them. It can be difficult. There are three responses: firstly,
try to explain to your partner what you are doing and why you
want to do it – if you can get your partner 'on board', they can

deal with their family; secondly, try to develop a thick skin for comments from all those, including your partner, who don't understand what you are doing; resign yourself to the fact that this is a part of your life that your partner can't share – there is plenty that you can enjoy together, but this is something for you; or thirdly, like Rita and Denny, go your separate ways:

Frank: . . . What's that?

Rita: It's me case.

Frank: Where are you going?

Rita: Me mother's.

Frank: What's wrong? . . .

Rita: I got home from work, he'd packed me case. He said either I stop comin' here an' come off the pill or I could get out altogether . . . It was an ultimatum. I explained to him. I didn't get narked or anythin'. I just explained to him how I had to do this. He said it's warped me. He said I'd betrayed him. I suppose I have . . . But I couldn't betray meself.

(W. Russell, 1986, p. 209)

Even with your partner's support and understanding, your PhD is likely to have an effect on your relationship. I moved home and got married during my PhD; but I didn't want to think about starting a family until I had got my doctorate. There are parts of your life which have to go on hold. And there are sacrifices in terms of the time you can spend with your partner – particularly in the last few months as you draw everything together and prepare to take your thesis for binding (see Chapter Eight).

Charles Campbell's wife reflected that he was 'a nightmare to live with' during his research. For partners of PhD students, my husband has this advice: 'Just listen. There is no point in trying to offer solutions.' As a PhD student you won't be looking to your partner for practical solutions, unless they too are a PhD student or have their own PhD. Instead, you'll want emotional support. You sometimes need to be allowed just to talk – out loud. This can help your brain to process information and you to work through issues. Tobias Feakin agrees that 'because you are researching and writing about such specialized areas, there are few others who understand what you are doing'.

'Will somebody think of the children?'

Just as your PhD impacts upon your life and the way you live it, so too can life impact upon your PhD and how you manage to conduct your research. What if I had got pregnant during my research? Could I have completed my PhD? Pregnancy didn't happen to me, but it has happened to other students. Under the terms of my studentship I was entitled to take 26 weeks maternity leave. There is provision for women to take a break from their studies to have a baby; or you can apply for an interruption in your registration, if you haven't got a contract with a clause allowing maternity leave. You can also apply for an interruption in your registration for paternity leave if you are about to become a dad.

So in theory having a baby is not a problem, although in practice you will need to be extremely determined, having had a baby, to pick up where you left off and continue with your PhD. If taking a new job during your PhD is a side show that interests and distracts you, having a baby is like a West End musical that demands your full attention from the start. Getting your research back on track may be more difficult than you imagine. You may find that what you used to think was important (your PhD), no longer has the same meaning or relevance in your life. If you *are* determined to re-engage with it, there are two key issues: the need for childcare, and the fact your brain has turned into mashed potato. But the latter is temporary, and in my experience, starting to use my brain again as soon as possible seemed to help.

I remember the first newspaper article I wrote, eight weeks after my son was born. I had to draft it three times! It took two days of extremely laborious effort. But after this watershed, writing seemed to get easier, and eventually became a more natural and less forced process. What *did* get more difficult was finding time to write as baby slept less during the day. Jo Brand and Mel Giedroyc are celebrity mothers who have both written books since the birth of their children (Brand, 2004, 2005;

Giedroyc, 2006). Talking about writing her first novel, *Sorting Out Billy*, Brand has said, 'It was great, it fitted in with my life at the time as I have two young kids so I needed to stay at home, to save my husband being on his own with them and going mentally ill. It was easy to run upstairs, chain them to a radiator and get on with it' (J. James, 12 May 2004).

'Yes,' I thought when I was contemplating this book, 'I'll write between seven and nine each evening.' I hadn't realized that by seven in the evening all I would want to do was pour a large glass of wine, collapse onto the sofa, and gaze at the television. Nor did I realize that by then, after a good few hours of children's TV, I had the mind of a Teletubby. Can you organize some childcare during the day for your tot? Sixteen hours a week may be enough for a humanities student – if you have to do lab work, you'll need more. But you'll have to be determined: not that it's an impossible task, just a challenging one.

In terms of finance, if you have a studentship you may be entitled to statutory maternity/paternity pay; check the terms of your contract. For women, the Department for Work and Pensions won't regard your bursary as earnings for the purpose of claiming Maternity Allowance – this is what the government pays mothers who are employed and earning at least £30 a week, but do not qualify for statutory maternity pay from their employer. Maternity Allowance is paid at the same rate as Statutory Maternity Pay but is paid by the government, not your employer. If you are working part-time while completing your research, you may qualify for Maternity Allowance. You can get full details from your local Job Centre Plus, or online at the Department for Work and Pensions website (www.dwp.gov.uk).

If you don't qualify for Maternity Allowance you may be entitled to other benefits, such as Incapacity Benefit. Talk to an advisor at your own institution, or at your Job Centre Plus, to see if you can claim any financial support – new dads should do likewise.

Having children already is no bar to completing a PhD. Look at Hattie's comments at the start of this book: she wished she had begun her PhD research earlier. If your youngest child has just started school, it may be the ideal time to start. A PhD studentship in a humanities subject usually allows flexibility, and if you're not used to earning a wage and can get a studentship, the bursary will be a bonus.

Reading

I know a single mum who is doing her PhD; her children are at the top end of primary school. She also works full-time. I take my hat off to her! She explains clearly to her children, 'I have to go and do this reading – I'll be back to make your tea in an hour. If you get hungry in the meantime, make yourselves some noodles.' I imagine them all sitting down together to do their 'homework'. There's no getting away from it, you'll have to do a lot of reading, and whatever your circumstances you'll have to carve out time to do it.

I never really enjoyed reading before my PhD. I would have preferred an amanuensis to read for me, and tell me what they had read. But I have learned to love reading. I have certainly read more during and since my PhD – both for research and for pleasure – than I did during my previous 24 years. I remember that at secondary school, at the end of each year we would have to fill in a self-assessment sheet for English. The goals I set myself were the same each year – to read more, and improve my spelling.

I spent my first term at Goldsmiths adjusting to being a full-time researcher, and reading relevant literature. Now I can talk easily about reading relevant literature, completing a literature review, and compiling a bibliography. But at the time, I was anxious: 'Where do I find "relevant literature", and how will I know when I've read all of it?'

Reading is an issue for many students. Your supervisor should be able to advise you on the most important journals in your field. To start locating reading on a specific topic, search a bibliographic database. There will be a subject librarian in your university library who can show you how to do this. If you begin your PhD at the start of the academic year, it's quite likely you'll be given a library tour as part of your induction. If you begin at another point in the year, seek out the subject librarian and introduce yourself. Once you've found several relevant books and journal articles, you can follow up the literature cited. As you continue, you'll find yourself increasingly 'tuned in' to your study. There is much to be said for the *serendipity* of research. I found a fantastic book by Erna Paris (2002) on a stand in Belfast airport on the way home from a friend's wedding in Ireland. You may also just happen to come across relevant material. This is because your PhD is with you all the time, in your mind's eye, and so you're always on the lookout for relevant sources. Suddenly, items on the radio and programmes on the television have an unexpected relevance. As you talk to other people in your field, they may also suggest references for you.

Like many PhD students, I wanted to read everything I could to make sure I had 'positioned myself' in my research, and knew everything about the topic before I started any fieldwork. But at some point, the reading has to stop. Unlike in medieval times, when perhaps a reader could cover all the books written on any one subject, the amount of literature on any single topic is so overwhelming now that no one could read it all. Taking my area of research, for example, the standard bibliography of works on the Nazi period stood at 25,000 in 1995 and 37,000 in 2000 (Evans, 2003, p. xvi). That reflects an average increase of 2,400 new items a year. I couldn't possibly read the entire bibliography, or hope to keep up with that volume of annual output. Professor Felipé Fernandez-Armesto has written about this in a volume edited by Professor David Cannadine, *What is History Now?* (2002). Fernandez-Armesto talks about the growth of scholarly output as a result of the technological revolution. The sheer volume of output has led to greater and greater specialization, so that even experts in their field may not know of every relevant work. And increased output means more rubbish, as well as more good stuff! But Fernandez-Armesto concludes that 'it is bliss to be alive in a dawn such as ours'. Though you could read and read and still not have read everything relevant to your subject.

So read as much as you can, but don't even try to read everything – you'll never be able to. It's more important to start writing as soon as possible, since this helps you to formulate your ideas about what you have read. I read for the whole of my first term. Then I started to write, alongside my continued reading of relevant literature.

Note-taking

I should perhaps put a note in here about notebooks and keeping track of your reading. I hope it doesn't sound patronizing. I know a senior lecturer who, the day before she was submitting her thesis, was in a London library on her mobile phone to her husband, who was thumbing through her thesis and reading out to her a list of missing references. In theory we all know we should keep a note of all our references; but I am willing to bet you'll be chasing one or two references just before you take your thesis for binding. I was on maternity leave (my baby and I arrived home on the same day as a fat manila envelope from my publisher) when the proofs for my first book arrived, along with a list of queries. I had to email librarians at various institutions, begging them to check references for me. And I had been pretty good at keeping a note of my reading! Throughout my PhD I worked with three A5 notebooks. One was for my journal. One I kept with me, to jot down ideas that occurred to me out of the blue, details of interesting radio and television programmes, and references that were recommended to me.

The third one I used with a computer program for managing bibliographies. In this notebook I wrote down my references, giving each its own reference number (so I could cross-reference between my notebook and the computer program) and keeping a note of the date for that entry. In case I wanted to read the reference again later, I also wrote down where I had borrowed it from, or whether it was my own copy. Then I would make any relevant notes from the reading and write out quotations that I thought I might want to use.

I only kept my journal for the first two terms. After that, I settled into my studies and became more confident. I wish I'd kept it up, though. Ashley Smith Hammond kept a blog for a term during her final year of study, as a 'gesture of solidarity' with her students who had been asked to keep a diary as part of the course she was teaching. It may seem we were making work for ourselves, but a journal or blog provides a good place for reflection. Ashley's students were supposed to use their diaries to 'set goals, think through what it will take to meet your goals, and then look back and see how and if you managed to meet your goals'. The enormity of completing a PhD can sometimes seem insurmountable. Ashley quotes in one of her blog entries the old joke about how to eat an elephant: a bit at a time! Breaking down what you need to do into parts, and setting yourself goals and deadlines – for example, a list of things 'to do by week ending …' – are good ideas. Keeping these notes in one place means you've got written evidence of your progress, particularly useful when the gremlins are telling you you haven't made any at all – you've just sat and eaten jelly babies all day.

Upgrading and publishing papers

Initially all students enrol on an MPhil programme, and apply later to upgrade to PhD status. Usually at this point you go through a mini-viva where two members of your department (but not your supervisor) consider whether you are working at the appropriate level for a PhD. This 'upgrade' (which is much less terrifying than the upgrade process carried out by the Cybermen in *Dr Who*, and much less terrifying than the viva itself) usually takes place about halfway through your study. It is usually a formality. You will probably have to submit two chapters, including the literature review if you write one, along with a bibliography. Your department should have guidelines about how to present your work, and who to submit it to. I found the upgrade a positive experience. It is good to get feedback on your research, and reassurance that you're heading in the right direction. I found it helpful to talk about my work with academics not directly involved: their questions, and our discussion, made a helpful contribution to my writing. In one chapter I had included a quote about the teaching of history from Margaret Thatcher's memoirs:

> History is an account of what happened in the past. Learning history, therefore, requires knowledge of events. It is impossible to make sense of such events without absorbing

sufficient factual information and without being able to place
matters in a clear chronological framework – which means
knowing dates. No amount of imaginative sympathy for
historical characters or situations can be a substitute for the
initially tedious but ultimately rewarding business of
remembering what actually happened.

(Thatcher, 1993, p. 595)

This quotation was sandwiched between an extract from the
History Working Group's minutes about assessing history, and
a quotation from Martin Kettle about how the Conservative
government of the day had realized that there was a major issue
at stake concerning the National Curriculum for History:

Margaret Thatcher has fought many historic battles for what
she sees as Britain's future. Few of them, though, are as
pregnant with meaning as her current battle for control over
Britain's own history ... The debate is a surrogate for a much
wider debate about the cultural legacy of the Thatcher years.
It is about the right to dissent and debate not just history but
a range of other assumptions. If the Prime Minister can
change the way we are taught history, she will have succeeded in changing the ground rules for a generation to
come. It is a big prize.

(Kettle, 1990)

I was trying to make a point about Thatcher's view of school
history, and how I saw this as flawed, but one of the academics
involved in my upgrade said: 'I found myself agreeing with
Margaret Thatcher's view.' I hadn't given enough background
or framed my argument clearly. I spelled out the point more
clearly in my final draft: the quotation from Thatcher's memoirs was followed by more on her view of history, then a
paragraph arguing my case:

During Prime Minister's Question Time on 29 March 1990,
John Stokes MP asked:

Is my Right Hon. Friend aware that there is considerable
anxiety about the teaching of English history in our schools?
Instead of teaching only what are called themes, why cannot

we go back to the good old days when we learnt by heart the names of the kings and queens of England, the names of our warriors and battles and the glorious deeds of our past?

The Prime Minister replied that:

As usual, my Hon. Friend is absolutely right. What children should be taught in history is the subject of vigorous debate. I agree with him. Most of us are expected to learn from experience of history, and we cannot do that unless we know it. Children should know the great landmarks of British history and should be taught them at school.
(Hansard, H. of C., Vol. 170, Col 668, 29 March 1990)

It could be argued that history as perceived in this sense, without procedural concepts such as historical evidence and explanation, may be better described as antiquarianism. Even if history is about content alone, Thatcher's perception of the subject is perhaps questionable since, as I made clear in Chapter Two [of my thesis], history is not static. New historical evidence and different methodologies mean that our understanding and interpretation of historical events and personalities are revised. History is a discipline which is constantly growing and developing. Kettle has suggested that for the Conservatives the debate surrounding the National Curriculum for History was not about what history is; he suggests that in fact they had realized that there was something much bigger at stake . . .
(L. Russell, 2005, p. 93)

I remember being surprised that the other academic at my upgrade seemed more interested in the couple of typos I'd made than in the content of my writing. But those mistakes shouldn't have been there! My lead supervisor always emphasized that it was a frustrating waste of time to have to make typing corrections to your thesis if it could otherwise have been passed straightaway. Since the upgrade is a mini-viva, I should have been more careful.

Chapter Three

Pen to paper

At Goldsmiths, the 'spring review week' in the first year helps research students to prepare for their upgrade. I had to give a 'spring presentation', essentially telling the story of my research: what had motivated me to propose my research project? What research methods was I proposing to use? What had I done so far? And what was I going to do next? The response to my presentation from the PhD students and the academics in the audience was positive. This boosted my confidence.

Opportunities like this are good practice for giving conference papers. Some students think they shouldn't give papers or publish any of their research before they have their viva – but examiners like to see you have done these things. So it's a good idea to publish a paper after your upgrade. You don't get paid for publishing an article in an academic journal but it gives you kudos, particularly if you get a paper published in a 'peer review' journal. In that case, the paper you submit is sent to at least two academics who are experts in the field. They act as referees: they scrutinize and comment on your paper, and suggest to the editor whether it should be published. This is all done anonymously – they won't know who you are, and you won't know who has reviewed your paper. There are guidelines for submission on most journals' websites which cover requirements, ethics, copyright, and the mechanics of submitting a paper.

As regards copyright, you shouldn't worry about not being able to publish a book based on your thesis after your viva, if you've already published material from the thesis. Publishers, like viva examiners, are more impressed if you've already published work. This shows that there's some interest in your work, and perhaps a market for it. Of course you can't keep reproducing the same work, but you'll be presenting the same material differently in a thesis, a journal article, a newspaper or magazine feature, or a book. You'll be writing for different audiences, with different purposes. Scholarly writing is more remote, aiming to examine an issue, present evidence, and get under the surface. This is very different from journalistic writing, which needs to be punchier and to grab the reader's attention immediately. Magazine and newspaper articles need to put over a message succinctly. You must have something to say: it doesn't have to be much, but you need to *say* something. Books allow for more invention, discussion, and imagination. There is more space in a book, and your writing will be 'softer' than in a magazine or an academic journal.

Writing your thesis

Three years (or six if you are part-time) seems like a long time when you first start out. But it isn't, as Dr Michael Corbett notes:

> The first year you don't really get going, then during the second year and into the third you find yourself more pre-occupied with the subject. It's a bit like starting to figure out a complex puzzle. Thoughts blend across the 'study/personal life' barrier. By the time you hit that third year and then the thesis-writing at the end, it can be really intense, mentally and emotionally. And I did go temporarily mad. I can even tell you when it started.

> It was 1 October 2000, the start of my fourth year on the PhD. It hit like a ton of bricks ... You don't consciously make a deadline but it's there intrinsically in the process, and then the stress suddenly appeared – and with force.

So you need to keep to a timetable if you want to finish in three years, and it helps to have a series of goals you want to achieve, with deadlines you've set yourself. A journal is also a good place to write about how you're feeling: What's bothering you? What's going well? The journal helps you get things off your chest, especially if there's no one around you can talk to. While you're writing, you're also thinking problems through or congratulating yourself on a job well done. Your journal might also provide a good 'displacement activity'.

I sat down at my computer ten minutes ago. Since then, I've checked my emails and visited various websites. These are my displacement activities, and this paragraph is the first I've written today. I can only write when I'm in the right frame of mind, and as you see I prepare to work by means of my own displacement activities. Others have to make a space to work in, so they start by tidying their desk.

But, as Hattie says, your PhD is always with you. It takes over your life. You don't have to be sitting at a desk to be working on your thesis. Often, when you are doing daily tasks like loading the washing machine or putting out the rubbish, you are thinking about your work. J.K. Rowling wrote on her website in September 2006: 'I am currently trying to decide between two possible titles [for the seventh and final *Harry Potter*]. I was quite happy with one of them until the other one struck me while I was taking a shower in New York.' I have had similar flashes of inspiration while taking a shower. But the title for *this* book came to me during a train journey. (Rowling first came up with the idea for *Harry Potter* on a train. But there the parallels between her huge literary success, and my own work, undoubtedly end).

The first draft of your thesis is the hardest. And trying to write alongside reading relevant journal articles, theses and books makes the process more difficult. When you read what someone else has written, self-doubt creeps in again: 'This is really good. I can't write like this!' Stuart Foster told me of the endless hours he was spending

> reading heavy-going academic papers and textbooks, trying to relate what I read to the data and then writing up. In spite of the seemingly endless tweaking, re-writing, adding and amending, I'm never really sure that the product of my labours really cuts the mustard academically, as the writers I am reading appear so far ahead of me.

Dr John Lunnun also said that he continually questioned his 'ability to write at the academic level like the articles and books' he was reading. Not everyone can. There are a few who are counselled off PhD programmes because they can't quite make the jump from MA level. But they are just a few. When you're reading journal articles and books, it's important to remember that what you are reading is a construct; it's the polished version, work that has been written and rewritten, edited and re-edited. The first draft of this book was very different from what you are reading now. It doesn't matter what you think about your writing, because no one else will read it unless you want them to. Writing is a continuous process. The important thing is to get the first draft done, then you've got something to work with. And you don't have to do it in one go: if you do some writing and leave it for a few days, when you come back and start editing and extending it you'll probably think, 'Actually, this is pretty good.'

The first piece I wrote was the basis of my introductory chapter, in which I 'situated myself' in the research (see Chapter Five). I was pleased to start writing. On the whole, I enjoy it. Others find writing a more difficult experience and prefer reading and doing their research project. There was a fellow PhD student (who I mention in the following chapter) who was of this persuasion. She was always busy at her computer when I got into college. I forgive her for never coming with me for coffee! Writing up requires self-discipline, especially when you have set yourself the task of writing your entire thesis in a matter of months. But having been out of academia for three years, and not having done a Masters degree, it was important for me to practise academic writing. My former pupils would tell me after a lesson of role play and group-work, when they learned a lot but only wrote a little, 'That was a really good lesson, Miss. We didn't have to do any work!' Like them, I felt I was only working if I was writing. Written work was physical evidence of my endeavours. But it is not uncommon for some PhD students to wait until the end of their study, when they've read everything they wanted to and finished their research project, before they start to write. That approach may work for them, but it wouldn't for me.

Creme and Lea (1997) identify four types of writer: the *diver* writer just plunges into their work, and needs to do some writing to find out what they want to say. The *patchwork* writer initially writes in sections, and then links the sections together to construct their argument. The *grand plan* writer spends a lot of time reading and thinking then sits down knowing what they are going to write, and writes it without the need for redrafting. The *architect* writer makes a plan with headings in mind, knowing the broad structure of their writing before they produce the content (Creme and Lea, 1997, pp. 79–83). The description of the 'grand plan' writer fits how Professor Clyde Chitty works: while walking his dogs in the morning, he composes his writing in his mind. When he gets home he writes out in longhand what he has prepared mentally. I am naturally a 'diver' writer, but during my PhD I was also sometimes a 'patchwork' or 'architect' writer. I drafted and redrafted the chapters of my thesis.

The first chapter I wrote after my introduction was to become the third chapter in my thesis, 'Issues surrounding teaching the Holocaust in history'. It is the hardest piece of writing I have ever done. The chapter examined the issue of terminology. As I have noted in Chapter One, I didn't write a literature review as such. But before I began, like every other PhD student I needed to position myself in the research, and review and analyse relevant literature. I wanted to write about terminology early on, so that I was clear in my own mind what I meant by particular terms. If you take the title of my thesis, 'Teaching the Holocaust in school history; policy and classroom perspectives' (L. Russell, 2005), an issue immediately arises (ripe for cross-examination on the day of the viva!): why has 'holocaust' got a capital 'h'? What was *the* Holocaust? What is meant by the term? There are a multitude of definitions. While some historians and authors used the term to refer to the treatment of all of the victims of German National Socialism, others used it exclusively to describe the Jewish experience. I needed to outline the different definitions, and state which one I was using and why.

And this was not all: there are related questions and implications, such as what and who does the term 'Holocaust' encompass? Is the term 'holocaust' actually appropriate to describe the suffering, persecution and murder of Jews in Hitler's Germany? Was the term 'Shoah' (a Hebrew word meaning 'a great and terrible wind', pronounced 'sho-wah') more appropriate? The literature also debated whether or not the Holocaust was a unique event. Could the term be used to describe other examples of genocide?

The amount of debate and literature about these questions is massive. Wading through the reading and producing a piece of writing outlining the issues was both exhausting and necessary. I remember sitting at my kitchen table (snowed under by books and papers), with numerous ideas circulating in my mind. Somehow I had to synthesize all this – the arguments and the viewpoints – and explain my position to my readers. I wrote and rewrote the same few sentences endlessly, trying to find the right opening lines. This is not an uncommon problem. Dr Christine Poulson is an academic and novelist. Describing writing in a piece for the *Times Higher Education Supplement*, Christine says, 'This morning nothing goes right. I type a sentence. I delete it and try again. I delete that and reinstate the first sentence. It's still no good. I seem to have forgotten how to do this' (Poulson, 2004).

I had to bear in mind that although I was very familiar with the subject matter, much of it would be new to the reader. So I needed to construct my thesis in an intelligible way, signposting the points I was making and taking my readers along with me. I sat for hours staring at the sentences I had started to write, and then abandoned. I was tying myself in knots, and in a state of mental paralysis. The problem was that I knew what I had to get down on the paper in front of me – but turning abstract thoughts into coherent words was extremely difficult. I did a lot of thinking. I reread some of the books and articles. I emailed friends involved in Holocaust education . . . and I finally put the words on the page.

Dr Charles Campbell describes his experience of writing up thus:

> The writing I had begun as a diversion had taught me one invaluable lesson: changing something – anything – is easier than producing a sentence from scratch. It is all too easy to spend a week staring at a flashing cursor, attempting to conjure up that killer, all-absorbing, first line.

I eventually constructed an initial draft. Having done so, I was clearer about my own ideas and how to tackle the practical part of my research project. It's easy to put off writing, because getting started is always daunting. But I would have found it impossible to have waited until I had completed my research to sit down with piles of notebooks, a blank page, and more than 50,000 words to write. Where to begin? For me, reading, practical research, teaching and writing cannot be separated out and completed sequentially or in isolation. The processes feed off, and merge into, one another. As for Charles, things started to improve when he changed his approach to the PhD process:

> At my lowest point, somewhere around 18 months into my research, things did begin to change. I made a concerted effort to engage in more beyond my basic research: I started writing popular science articles for a magazine, took undergraduate tutorials, and taught for a week in a secondary school. And then my research finally began to come together – a trickle of results, then a steady flow.

I wrote regularly for the *Times Educational Supplement* during my research, as well as teaching on teacher education programmes at college. These related activities were both a diversion from my PhD research, and an opportunity to talk about what I was doing, to the people I was doing it for: other teachers. Talking about your work – out loud – and explaining concisely what you are doing, and why, can be very helpful. Somehow, it helps you to understand what you're trying to do; clarifies your ideas; and sharpens your focus. The responses and questions from your audience can enhance your work. Research groups can be useful in the same way, but some of them are, as John Lunnun notes, 'a little precious at times'. In Charles's circumstances – where he didn't seem to be making any progress – working *less* hard on his PhD made the difference. A work–life balance is important. Charles benefited from writing articles and teaching, and then found a further boost to his work:

A new post-doc joined the group and we very quickly became firm friends and faced down the challenges together. It was by far the most productive and happiest period of my studentship, and it left me wondering what it might have been like had I had just a little more support throughout. Over the ensuing months I collected a wealth of data. Then, with approximately two months of funding left, I confronted the prospect of transforming my new-found knowledge into a thesis. For that, I required peace and quiet. It would herald a return to long, lonely days, this time in a spare room at home. But by that time I had a new-found confidence, and writing the thesis was a component of my PhD which I suspected I might enjoy ... I adhered to a strict personal routine: I got up when my girlfriend got up to go to work, took an hour for lunch with a 30-minute power nap, and worked on until she got home in the evening. Evenings and weekends were strictly reserved for us. It was not necessarily a régime that would suit everybody, but it worked for me.

There is no single 'right' way of working. I wrote in fits and starts, one week 7,000 words, the next 3,000, and another week none. There are writers – like Philip Pullman – who write 1,000 words a day. Alexander McCall Smith (who himself has a PhD, and is a professor of medical law) has written over 70 books including academic texts, novels and children's stories. He told the *California Literary Review* in February 2005:

> When I am busy with the day-to-day tasks of being an author – book signings, talks, etc. – I have to snatch short spells of time in which to write. Sometimes this can be on planes or in hotel rooms, as I travel on promotional tours. When, however, I have the opportunity to spend large chunks of my time on my writing I will write for more than four hours a day, more or less without stopping.
> (www.calitreview.com/Interviews/int_smith_8008.htm)

In an interview with *Bookends* (published online at www.thebookplace.com/bookends), McCall Smith explained that when he was at home he liked 'to write early in the morning. *Scotland Street*, the novel I write in daily episodes through the pages of *The Scotsman* newspaper, is very good discipline. I need to write 1,000 words a day for this.' He further described his preferred writing environment and routine in his newsletter of July 2007:

> My real choice of writing-place would be my house in Edinburgh. When I am at home, as I am now, I have a very pleasant routine of writing in the morning, a siesta, and then more work later on. I write in my study, which is a large room filled with books, and looking west. From there I am immediately transported mentally to the place that I am writing about – to Botswana, perhaps, to those landscapes that mean so much to Mma Ramotswe, to those wide plains and that high, empty sky. And it's almost as if they're there with me in the room – Mma Ramotswe, Mma Makutsi, and Mr J.L.B. Matekoni – all with me, waiting for me to chronicle the latest developments in their lives. It's like having friends – good friends who are always ready for a cup of tea and talk when you are.
>
> (McCall Smith, 7 August 2007)

Writing requires discipline and, to some extent, routine. Anthony Horowitz's website informs us that he 'is perhaps the busiest writer in England'. He is indeed prolific: his writing credits include his *Alex Rider* books; episodes of *Poirot*, *Murder in Mind*, *Midsomer Murders* and *Murder Most Horrid*; and the TV series *Foyle's War*. Horowitz 'writes in a comfortable shed in his garden for up to ten hours a day' (http://www.anthonyhorowitz.com/about/). It is worth finding a place you find comfortable and conducive for writing, and having some sort of writing routine that you stick to even if you don't think you have got anything to write about. You may not know when you sit down what you are going to write about, but you need to give inspiration the chance to strike.

As a writer, C.J. Sansom uses his professional background (he has a PhD in history and was a lawyer until he began writing full-time), and Christine Poulson (who is based at Sheffield University) does likewise: her crime novels have an academic setting. She says that once she has 'begun a draft it's important to keep going'. When writing her novel *Footfall* she aimed at '4,000 words a week spread over four mornings'. For your writing, 1,000 words a day is an excellent target. But don't be frustrated if you don't hit this target every day. Christine reports, in her *Don's Diary* for the *Times Higher Education Supplement*, that 'by one o'clock I've written less than 300 words. A friend comes for lunch. Whether it's the conversation or the glass of wine, I don't know, but when my daughter falls asleep, I write 700 words' (Poulson, 2004). Sometimes you need a break.

Some authors know exactly what they are going to write, then they sit down and write it. I usually have some idea what I want to write, but my thoughts develop when I'm at my computer or at the kitchen table, sharp pencil in hand. I usually write in longhand and then type it up, but sometimes I think more clearly at the computer. I like to stop writing before I've completely finished a piece of work, so I have somewhere to start next day.

It doesn't matter if you don't write anything for a short time. Sometimes you need to mull over ideas; you might be feeling uninspired, and need a longer break; or you might need to do some more research.

And don't feel guilty about making a cup of tea and watching the television for half an hour ... (or more!)

Chapter Four

What is a 'paradigm'?

'I've just been up to the desk. They're saying . . .'

'What, what are they saying?'

'That next information is at 16.30.'

'Oh, God . . .'

'It's inaccurate of course . . .'

'What is?'

'. . .as a credible communication. The word 'next' is implying a sequence, a continuum, and as yet no information of any significance has been conveyed so the use of the word 'next' is an indicator of . . .'

'What? What are you talking about?'

'Sorry.'

'I have no idea what you are talking about.'

'Probably for two reasons. I work in higher education . . .'
(Salon, 'Delayed Departures', *Afternoon Play*, BBC Radio 4)

You might think that as educated people academics should be able to communicate with others. It isn't always so. Academic language can be off-putting. It shouldn't be incomprehensible. The starting point for any PhD student is 'positioning themselves' in the research, which involves reviewing the literature on their chosen topic. But rather than being an enjoyable and interesting endeavour, this can be an intimidating and heavy-going experience. Here is an extract from the journal I kept while I was researching my PhD:

I have been told I must read some books about educational theory. Although some of the writing is good and interesting, I am becoming increasingly frustrated with the chapter I am reading. It is making me feel stupid. I am holding on to the thought that I can name several academics from different disciplines whose work I can read and understand perfectly well. If people want their ideas to be read about and acted upon, they should write in such a way as to make their text readable, accessible, enjoyable and interesting. That is good writing. The chapter I am reading, on the other hand, seems to have been written by someone who wishes to appear intelligent and only to further their own academic career. I don't like reading it. I am scared of it. I don't think I am clever enough to understand it.

Have just remembered a lecture given by one of the professors in the Sociology Department, in which new PhD students were told not to feel stupid or unworthy of 'The Academy'. If we don't understand something, it is because *it's badly written*.

(PhD Journal entry, January 2002)

Good communication is important – especially if you've discovered something which you want people to know about. I can't remember what I was reading that evoked this response. On reflection, my journal entry might not have been completely fair. You will probably meet people who are more intelligent and better-read than you, and they may have written a scholarly book. But if you, who are studying for a higher degree, can't understand what they have written, their ideas are not (in today's culture of soundbites and glossy presentation) going to have maximum impact. Being intelligent doesn't necessarily mean being good at communicating ideas. But perhaps a hard-to-understand work is not 'badly written' – it may not be written for a wider audience. How you write depends on what you think your research is *for*. For some academics, research is not about changing the world, so communicating their work to a wider audience is not a concern. In 'Old School Ties' – the second episode from the first series of *Lewis* – one of the characters (Stephen Gilchrist, played by Tom

Harper), an Oxford student, says to Inspector Lewis, 'I'm a scholar. I'd be happy to spend my life writing books that only 37 people in the world want to read.' (Planter, 2006).

As well as dealing with impenetrable academic text, I came across academics who could make me feel I didn't deserve my scholarship: 'Obviously we'd be working from a deficit because you don't have a Master's degree, so I can't talk "the language" with you.' Not the best introductory comment from a potential supervisor!

In Chapter One I wrote that having a PhD means: 'I am capable of designing and completing research, and am worthy of a university post.' Doing a PhD is also about proving oneself suitable for admission into a 'club'. It is a rite of initiation.

The late Mo Mowlam completed her doctoral research in the US state of Iowa in the 1970s. Her biographer Julia Langdon writes: 'There were not many women postgraduate students in the department. They were not made to feel particularly welcome either ... they all felt they were not taken seriously because they were women' (Langdon, 2000, p. 92). While things have changed in respect of the status of women in academia, the status of postgraduate students, and whether they feel welcome in their department, remains an issue. As a postgraduate it can feel as if you are 'in limbo' – neither an undergraduate nor a member of academic staff. Dr Alex Cousins said that this 'ambiguous position' was what she and her postgraduate colleagues found most difficult, and it led to some students feeling 'peripheral to the department and its activities'.

There may be academic snobbery among those who have doctorates. This usually disappears once you have passed the ritual of the viva, although you may still encounter some academics who do not view you as an equal. In the course of writing this book I invited various well-known academics to contribute 'a few sentences' on their experience of completing a PhD. I had one rather unhelpful reply from a well-known PhD who supervised students for many years, saying he/she 'had a good deal to say about how to go about writing a thesis and what a thesis is', but did not 'have the option of contributing "a few sentences"'. As in all walks of life, academia is full of different personalities.

To summarize: all workplaces have their own jargon, and doing a PhD is a rite of passage. However, academic snobbery exists and sometimes language is used to exclude. Whether intentional or not, language can make you feel isolated, and not just in academia. The BBC reported in November 2006 that one-third of the 3,000 workers polled in a survey about workplace jargon said they felt inadequate when wordy language was used there. Back at university, embarking on my PhD, I was struck by five words in particular: *problematic*; *equity*; *discourse*; *hegemony*; and *paradigm*. These words were used a lot. 'Problematic' was used (sometimes inexplicably) in place of 'a problem':

'I take my children to school before coming into work.'

'Oh, it's nice that you can do that.'

'Actually, it's quite problematic.'

'Equity' (equally inexplicably?!) seemed to be used in place of 'equality' or 'fairness': 'My work looks at issues of equity between boys and girls in the classroom'. Previously I only knew 'equitable' as part of the name of an insurance company. 'Discourse' is best defined as a 'way of understanding the world'. There is often talk of 'differing discourses' – different ways of understanding or seeing something. 'Hegemony' refers to a dominant idea. And a 'paradigm' means a framework or example. Not wanting to look stupid, I would smile and nod during conversations which included such terms, while noting them down phonetically so I could look them up later. Ashley Smith Hammond, in her final year of PhD research, wrote about vocabulary in her blog in February 2007:

> So I ended up going to a study day ... The first session was on ontology and epistemology – words that if I am honest I'm only kind of familiar with ... What are these crazy words, you ask me, what do they mean? Well, I'll quote from an article: 'Epistemology is the philosophical theory of knowledge, i.e. the study of knowledge. Ontology is the theory of the nature of being and existence, i.e. the study of being and existence. We create epistemological theories to support the ontological theories that we create' (Johnson,

2002). And if that quote doesn't make it any clearer then we can fall back on what I wrote in my notes on Friday, that ontologies are theories of reality – of how the world works.

It takes time to familiarize yourself with new terms. But in no time you'll find yourself 'engaging with a Foucauldian ontology' ...

What is truth?

Chapter Five focuses on this question, which relates to the issue of language. A piece in a church newsletter about 'truth' highlighted the issue of language and meaning. A friend of the writer, who was committed to telling the 'unadulterated truth', was asked what his reply would have been if he had been harbouring a Jew in occupied Holland during the Second World War, and Nazis came to the door asking: 'Do you know where any Jews are hiding?' He said he would have told the 'truth' and answered: 'Yes.' But the writer of the piece considered that he would have told the 'truth' by saying: 'No':

> It all depends on what the word Jew means. If by the word 'Jew' you mean a sub-human life form, only fit for the gas chambers, then you would have to answer 'Yes' to the question, to be telling the truth. But if you understood the word 'Jew' to mean a fully human being, deserving of all the dignities of any other human being ... then it would be perfectly acceptable to answer 'No' to the Nazi question without in any sense telling a lie.
>
> ('Our Faith on Sunday', 2006)

Me, myself and I

Regarding your own academic writing, perhaps the biggest issue is how you decide to refer to yourself. Or should that be *oneself*? As noted in the following chapter, it has become increasingly common in recent years for PhD theses to include a section of writing where the author situates themself in the research. I wrote an introductory chapter thus – the only chapter in which 'I' appeared in my thesis. How much of an issue this is depends on your discipline. The personal pronoun is becoming more common. Romona Tang and Suganthi John have written an interesting article about the use of 'I' in academic writing. This is from their abstract:

> Academic writing has traditionally been thought of as a convention-bound monolithic entity that involves distant, convoluted and impersonal prose. However, recent research has suggested a growing recognition that there *is* room for negotiation of identity within academic writing, and thus academic writing need not be totally devoid of a writer's presence. In this article, we explore the notion of writer identity in academic essays by focusing on first person pronouns, arguably the most visible manifestation of a writer's presence in a text. Our main argument is that the first person pronoun in academic writing is not a homogeneous entity.
>
> (Tang and John, 1999)

Many phrases can be used in place of 'I' – even without resorting to 'we' or 'the author' or 'one', which are also often inappropriate. 'One' and 'the author' sound a bit pretentious. But phrases like 'it could be argued that . . .' or 'the decision was made to . . .' are good alternatives.

It is important to maintain a neutral stance, and rely on the research to make your point: academic writing is very different from journalism, but it isn't easy to maintain the more controlled style you need for your work. Often the main obstacle is human emotion: you may feel excited about a particular point, and want to make the most of it. Dr John Lunnun was frustrated in this way. He says he was often reminded not to be 'too political' in his thesis, 'however I have always felt that academic neutrality can sometimes flatten a contention. I think I managed to keep an edge in it [the thesis] without too much frothing at the mouth'. One of my own difficulties with my methodology chapter – which I hated writing, and which is discussed in Chapter Six – was that I just didn't perceive it as exciting. And I wanted my writing to be exciting! But you have to do what is necessary to get your PhD, and that means taking 'a step back' from your work. Scholarly writing is about presenting your data to your audience, rather than describing what you think about your data. You can write a piece for a newspaper or magazine which is punchy and 'puts over your message'. But your thesis can't put over a message because this suggests that what you are saying is absolute. And, as is emphasized in the following chapter, there are few (if any) absolutes in academic research.

Language extends beyond the written and spoken word. I remember some PhD students who sometimes made me feel like a charlatan. I worked hard. But I also became familiar with the daytime television schedules. I did not work nine to five Monday to Friday. But every time I went into college (usually arriving mid-morning after my commute) there were a couple of fellow PhD students in the research centre, where they had been ensconced since 9am busily reading or writing. They would say 'hello', but barely turn away from their computer or book. They were busy. They were working hard. (Harder than me? Was I really good enough to be there? Would I get a PhD?) My usual response was to check my emails, and then turn on my heel and go and get a coffee. Of course, the hard workers were too busy to come with me. I wondered if they secretly felt like charlatans, as I did, and whether they really were working as hard as they seemed to be. Was this a façade, intended to give the 'right' impression? I still don't know. But one of these students decided, after five years of research and active involvement in his department, to abandon his career in academia. He didn't complete his thesis. I think the other just had a different way of working from me. Maybe she had to work flat-out in the final months, because she was writing her entire thesis at the end of her enrolment having first completed all of her research.

PhD students from other departments were cold comfort. There was one, a nice chap (the ones who do the most boasting tend to be male) who went on about his 'important' and 'groundbreaking' work (about the public transport system), and how he wanted to complete his thesis in 18 months: 'I'd like to get it done before the end of the minimum period of registration, and submit it as soon as possible.' I finished my work in three years exactly. I needed to, because after that my funding ran out. My graduation was a year later, and at the ceremony I was pleased to recognize a friendly face. Guess who? The same nice chap!

Spare a thought for Charles, in tears over breakfast but apparently confident and self-assured in the lab. However you feel inside, there is pressure to maintain a cool, calm and confident exterior. And maybe that isn't a bad thing – the pretence may stop you being utterly consumed by despair. But whenever you hear students boasting that they're going to finish their thesis in two years, or they've written three chapters in six weeks, ignore them. If they aren't putting up a front because they feel unworthy of the academy, then they'll probably be advised by their supervisor that what they have written will need re-writing. Maybe – if they're lucky – they've got the basis of three chapters!

I've got nothing to wear

There is also the language of clothes. What you wear says who you are, or who you want to be. Think of the Spice Girls: Mel C and Victoria Beckham told us they were 'Sporty' and 'Posh' by what they wore. For me, as a young teacher, dressing was easy: I wanted to look smart and authoritative while still looking my age. I didn't want to have to think about what to wear at 6.45am, or wear the clothes I wore at the pub at the weekend. So in the classroom, it was a trouser suit and a fashionable shirt; and footwear? A pair of heeled boots in the winter, and sandals in the summer. (Liam, the same student who asked me if I was going to become a 'doctor of dates', once asked me if teaching with my 'toes out' was a distraction.) This is what I wore to my PhD interview too. But the move back to academia meant abandoning this uniform. The question was, what to wear as a research student?

Although I felt a suit was too formal for my new role (even some of the senior lecturers wore jeans) I was still a professional, and I didn't feel comfortable in the jeans and tops I'd worn as an undergraduate – particularly at research group meetings. The 'right' clothes give you greater confidence, as Gok Wan has shown in his successful Channel 4 series, *How To Look Good Naked*. And during my first term as a research student, I needed my confidence boosting. So I went shopping.

There is something tribal about your wardrobe. All of us are attracted – at least initially – to people who dress in a similar way. At your first meeting with someone, what they're wearing tells you whether they might be your kind of person. I remember as an undergraduate discussing in a sociology seminar the power and symbolism of clothes: if yours are taken away and replaced with a gown when you become a hospital patient, your identity is taken away and you only have a role: 'patient'. The doctor wears a suit or a white coat; the nurses have uniforms. Doctors, nurses, patients: these are clearly defined hospital roles. But it was not so straightforward at my new institution. Who was I? Where did I fit in? Alex Cousins draws attention above to the issue of status and the postgraduate research student. How do you view your role and position? I think as a research student you need to find a look that you are comfortable with. I bought a cotton, khaki-coloured blazer and aimed at a 'smart casual' look for college and for conducting research interviews. But I could have stuck with my suit. I remember one fellow PhD student who was a very smart lady. She always wore a suit and make-up to college, and carried her research notes in a briefcase. She was comfortable – and confident. For most students, T-shirts and jeans are the order of the day – the best of these being reserved for teaching.

Call me doctor

Once you have your doctorate you are entitled to call yourself 'doctor'. But there is then the question, which is related to the issue of language, of whether or not you choose to use your title. Is it pretentious to have 'Dr' on your credit card and passport? Mine still say 'Miss'. My passport is due for renewal, but I am reluctant to use my title on it – I might be asked to attend a medical emergency on a plane! The term 'Doctor' has come to be associated with one who heals. Even Doctor Who is apparently called a doctor not because of his profound knowledge of time and space, but because he is 'The man who makes things better'. At least that is Saxon's (The Master's) interpretation in Series Three's *The Sound of Drums* (Teague, 23 June 2007).

There was some debate about the use of the title 'Doctor' by those who hold non-medical doctorates early in 2007, when Gillian McKeith agreed to stop using her title in advertisements for her television programmes and health foods. McKeith has a distance-learning PhD in holistic nutrition from the American Holistic College of Nutrition. The Advertising Standards Agency decided that adverts for her programmes and products were misleading because the college was not accredited by any recognized educational authority when she completed the course – and she does not have a general medical qualification. McKeith never claimed to be a medical doctor, but it was felt that the public might assume she is one (Gibson, 12 February 2007). So be prepared: once you have your PhD, you will often hear the question: 'But you're not a real doctor are you?' It's not quite fair, but Philip Hensher wrote in the *Independent* in February 2007:

> One of the curious facts about adult life is what a very negative impression tends to be left by people who use their non-medical doctorate in anything but an academic context. I'm sure if Ms McKeith had just come on our screens and told people to stop eating lardy buns and start eating a bit more salad, we would enjoy her work just as much without the reminder of her holistic-nutrition PhD.

> The reason is that, conventionally, only employed academics and medical doctors are permitted to call themselves 'doctor' without looking a bit of an idiot. It rather goes with the tendency to wear a bow tie as a signifier of berk-dom. It's always been a great puzzle why the Home Secretary likes to be referred to as 'Dr John Reid' [he has a PhD in economic history]; in a career of his distinction, you would have thought the doctorate was the least of it, and Gordon Brown is wiser not to use his in any circumstances.
>
> (The *Independent*, 13 February 2007)

I normally use my title only at work – although I also use it in situations where I feel I am being patronized and want to make a point.

Issues of status and identity are bound up with the question of whether non-medical PhDs should use their title. It's different for professors. They have a title they can use in daily life without 'looking a bit of an idiot'. It's an unambiguous term, and a more familiar title than 'doctor' in a non-medical context. 'Professor' denotes expertise in a particular field. Also, it's a term used in popular culture: I grew up with Professor Yaffle, the knowledgeable woodpecker from *Bagpuss*, and Professor Ross Geller from *Friends*. Children today are familiar with the title, thanks to *Harry Potter* and his teachers at Hogwarts. There is no danger of confusing the general public with the title 'professor'; no danger of being asked to deal with a heart attack or an unexpected birth on an aeroplane – unless, of course, he/she happens to be a professor of medicine!

I have thought about changing my title on my bank cards, and I would like to do so, after all I worked hard for my doctorate – why shouldn't I use it? It might not be fair, but I do wonder if Hensher isn't right in his assessment of the issue.

You've got nothing to prove

The written, spoken and body language of the academy can be intimidating. But remember: *you are worthy of the academy*, even if you don't always feel like it.

Doing a PhD is not just about acquiring knowledge: the process changes you as a person, and one of the ways it changes you is in your own use of language, which becomes more considered and precise. This in turn alters the way you hear language around you – news broadcasts, for instance. I was watching the BBC television news the other day, and found myself not thinking about the story being reported, but considering the words that had been spoken by the newsreader: 'The government has announced new plans to help win the war on terror.' Can you go to war against a concept? Is the government trying to defeat an emotion? My antennae are also finely tuned when I hear statistics: 'It was reported today that crime has fallen ...' Hmm, I wonder if it really has? The number of *reported crimes* may have fallen. 'The number of assaults on police officers rose last year ...' I wonder why? What is behind these statistics?

Peter Russian, Chief Executive of Investors in People Scotland remarked, with reference to a news report on workplace jargon, that 'using management jargon doesn't make you a good manager'. In the same way, using academic language does not prove you are an intelligent academic. If you're talking about 'differing discourses and a developing hegemony' because those words best explain your research, great. But please remember, you really don't *have* to start using 'problematic' instead of 'problem'!

'What? What are you talking about?'

'Sorry.'

'I have no idea what you are talking about.'

'Probably for two reasons, I work in higher education. I think . . .'

'I wouldn't be able to understand you? I'm a doctor. I'm a consultant. I work in a teaching hospital . . .'

(Matthew Salon, 'Delayed Departures', BBC Radio 4, 1 May 2007)

Chapter Five

Questions, questions ... does truth exist?

It is easy to become divorced from reality when you are writing a PhD. There is something of an existentialist nature about the process. Everything becomes a question. Every sentence you write in your thesis has to be considered, and every point referenced and supported. But more than that, you have extra time to read and think, and to generally contemplate the universe. For those with funding to do their research full-time, normal daily routines have been removed. The only structure to your day is designed and imposed by yourself. The '50 minute bell' – and all that that entails – is gone. I could wear my pyjamas all day, read and write until three in the afternoon, realize I hadn't eaten, make a peanut butter sandwich – and keep going. Although I had thought all this freedom would be immediately liberating, I felt like Rosencrantz or Guildenstern in Tom Stoppard's play *Rosencrantz and Guildenstern are Dead*. Stoppard uses Shakespeare's characters to explore philosophical ideas such as existentialism. (For more on existentialism try starting with Earnshaw, 2006.) This chapter is about how the PhD process can cast you adrift on a sea of confusion, doubt and despair – and how you can stop yourself from drowning by hanging on to your flotsam of reality.

'The only beginning is birth and the only end is death – if you can't count on that, what can you count on?' (Stoppard, 1968, p. 30). There were times, especially early on, when I felt this was all I *could* count on. In Stoppard's play, Rosencrantz and Guildenstern are utterly confused about their direction and purpose. And sometimes, so was I. Doing a PhD had taken me back to my 'A' Level English lessons:

'Cartesian scepticism?'

'Yes, it's the philosophical idea that we can't be sure about empirical knowledge because we might be dreaming or hallucinating, or we may be being deceived. For example, how do we know that this table is actually here? We can see it [teacher bangs on table], we can feel it, *but does it really exist*? If we leave the room, is the table still here, or does it cease to be?'

In the Wachowski brothers' film *The Matrix* (Wachowski and Wachowski, 1999), humans think they are leading a normal life; they believe they have families and relationships; that they go to work; and that they have a social life. But their world is an artificial reality controlled by sentient machines. Human beings are connected to 'the Matrix' by cybernetic implants. They are being deceived. Theirs is not a 'true' reality. Similarly, Truman's reality in the film *The Truman Show* (Weir, 1998) was designed and constructed for the purpose of creating a TV show. So, how do *we* know anything for certain? How do we know that *we* are not being deceived? Is our own experience of an event the same as anyone else's experience of the same event? In the words of Pontius Pilate, 'What is truth?' (John 18:38).

What is 'truth'?

A police officer working in the field of anti-terrorism recently said to me, 'If only we could be certain about the accuracy of lie detectors, we could just wire people up to the machine and ask them, "Are you a terrorist?".' Daytime chat shows – and the United States justice system – suggest that the polygraph machine (lie detector) actually works. If you suspect your partner of having an affair with your best friend, but you aren't certain, you can phone a daytime TV show, and have them both wired up to a lie detector to find out the truth! How many women have been told that such fears and suspicions are true, when actually their partner never slept with their best friend? And how many relationships have collapsed as a result? Andrew Stephen highlighted the shortcomings of the polygraph in an article for the *New Statesman* in 2006:

Did ex-Representative Mark Foley have sex with teenage male congressional pages? …Was Aldrich Ames, a senior CIA official in charge of analysing Soviet intelligence, actually a Soviet double agent? … Evidence is mounting that, far from being the infallible tools of world-beating American investigative procedures that Hollywood would have us believe, [lie detector tests] have actually been responsible for countless miscarriages of justice, and have ruined lives. [Ames] sailed through three polygraphs before the CIA discovered that he was actually one of the worst US traitors in history … And Foley? … I suspect a polygraph test would have a 50:50 chance of digging the truth out of him. As a thick-skinned and smooth-talking politician who lived decades pretending to be somebody he isn't, he would probably have cruised through like Ames.

(Stephen, 16 October 2006)

The issue of language and meaning is important. As I pointed out to my police officer friend: 'If the person you were talking to was convinced that what they had done was right – that they were a freedom fighter – then they could be involved in what you would call terrorist activity, but answer "no" truthfully.'

Remember the story from the church newsletter? The question 'Are you harbouring a Jew?' could truthfully be answered 'Yes' or 'No'.

So, does 'truth' exist?

Is there any such thing as 'historical truth'?

Keith Jenkins says that 'history is a discourse about, but categorically different from, the past' (1991, p. 7). Professor Clyde Chitty illustrates this point using the example of the Peterloo Massacre in 1819. Back for a moment to A level history.

The Peterloo Massacre of 16 August 1819 was the result of a cavalry charge into the crowd at a public meeting at St Peter's Field, Manchester. The meeting had been organized by the Manchester Patriotic Union Society, a political group which campaigned for parliamentary reform (universal suffrage, the secret ballot, annual parliaments) and the repeal of the Corn Laws – a price-fixing cartel which protected farmers' profits from cheap foreign imports, and kept bread prices artificially high. A sizeable crowd had gathered (contemporary estimates range from 30,000 to 150,000 people) to hear Henry Hunt speak about adult suffrage. What happened next is a matter of debate, but the result was the death of eleven people and injury to several hundred others. Some of those killed were Waterloo veterans (Marlow, 1969, p. 13). The memory of the French Revolution (1789–1799), and the fear of revolution spreading from Europe, are likely to have influenced the actions of those in authority.

Historians Norman Gash (1979) and E.P. Thompson (1968) have both written about the Peterloo Massacre. While neither takes issue with the facts – the date and place – Gash and Thompson have contrasting interpretations of this event. Gash sees it as an administrative blunder rather than a massacre:

> On 16 August occurred the confusion, errors and bloodshed at St Peter's Field. The magistrates decided to arrest Hunt on the hustings before he could speak. The size of the crowd, probably about 60,000, made the use of the military for this purpose necessary. By accident the local yeomanry arrived before the regular force of hussars. The yeomanry almost instantly got into difficulties from the denseness of the crowd, obstructions on the ground, and their own indiscipline. They were believed to be under attack, and the hussars were sent in to extricate them. When it was all over about a dozen people were dead or dying, some hundreds badly injured. The country was shocked at the news; and within a week 'Peterloo', the satiric title coined with reference to the government's other great military victory at Waterloo, had passed into the political vocabulary of the British nation. Simultaneously Lord Sidmouth expressed the thanks of the Prince Regent to the Manchester magistrates and the yeomanry for their 'prompt, decisive and efficient measures for the preservation of the public tranquility'.
>
> Peterloo was a blunder; it was hardly a massacre. Possibly half the deaths, probably even more of the non-fatal injuries, were among those who were trampled underfoot by horses and the crowd in the panic that ensued. The public

indignation was a mark both of the strong liberal feeling in the country and of the general restraint normally exercised by the authorities in dealing with large political assemblies. It was because Peterloo was uncharacteristic that it achieved notoriety. The magistrates had made two mistakes: in endeavouring to arrest Hunt at the meeting, and in sending in the amateur, unpopular and politically-minded Manchester and Salford Yeomanry ...

(Gash, 1979, pp. 94–5)

Thompson, on the other hand, views the event as part of a class war:

There are two points about Peterloo which have, somehow, become lost in recent accounts. The first is the actual bloody violence of the day. It really was a massacre ... But the panic was not (as has been suggested) the panic of bad horsemen hemmed in by a crowd. It was the panic of class hatred. It was the *Yeomanry* – the Manchester manufacturers, merchants, publicans, and shopkeepers on horseback – which did more damage than the regulars (Hussars) ...

There is no term for this but class war. But it was a pitifully one-sided war. The people, closely packed and trampling upon each other in the effort to escape, made no effort at retaliation until the very edges of the field, where a few trapped remnants – finding themselves pursued into the streets and yards – threw brick-bats at their pursuers. Eleven were killed or died from their wounds. That evening, on every road out of Manchester the injured were to be seen. The Peterloo Relief Committee had, by the end of 1819, authenticated 421 claims for relief for injuries received on the field (a further 150 cases still awaited investigation). Of these, 161 cases were of sabre wounds, and the remainder were injuries sustained while lying beneath the crowd or beneath the horses' hooves. More than 100 of the injured were women or girls.

(Thompson, 1968, pp. 752–4)

'Administrative blunder' or 'class war'? Which is the 'true' account? What really happened at St Peter's Field in

Manchester on 16 August 1819? Gash is a conservative historian and former Professor of Modern History at the University of St Andrews. He is perhaps best known for his two-volume biography of Robert Peel (Gash, 1961, 1972). Thompson was a prominent post-war British Marxist historian. The convictions of each historian are unwittingly revealed on the pages of their texts.

Jenkins writes that 'The past has gone and history is what historians make of it' (1991, p. 8). His argument is that history books do not give us a 'true' account of the past, but only the bare facts about past events and characters, differently interpreted by historians. This is a post-modern view which argues that history is a branch of literature and that the 'narratives' of historians are like novels: what historians write is their own invention, based on texts which have come into being through an arbitrary process of human invention, in which every reader finds their own meaning (see Evans, 2002, pp. 6–7). The work produced by Gash and Thompson, as well as popular historians like David Starkey, would not be popular among post-modern historians because their style is literary and expresses their interpretation, rather than being written report style.

History Professor Sir Geoffrey Elton (who was David Starkey's supervisor during his PhD research on Tudor history at Cambridge University) claimed that post-modernist theory was 'the intellectual equivalent of crack'. Elton wrote, 'we are fighting for the lives of innocent young people beset by devilish tempters who claim to offer higher forms of thought and deeper truths and insights' (Elton, 1991). This debate was at its height in the 1980s. But many criticisms of history as a discipline voiced by post-modernists had already been considered by professional historians. For example, David Harlan said that historical texts could no longer be regarded as having the fixed and unalterable meaning given them by their author.

But R.J. Evans questions whether historians had ever believed that meaning can be fixed in this way (Evans, 1997, p. 103). And in successive editions of his book *The Nature of History*, Arthur Marwick has stressed the importance of using language as clearly and precisely as possible, in order to avoid misunderstanding and misrepresentation. He insists that historians should try hard to keep their politics and prejudices out of their historical writing (2001, p. 7). There is more on this below.

Do I exist?

Reading about philosophical ideas like post-modernism is necessary for positioning yourself and your research. But I found that if I stayed too long on this higher intellectual plane I began to feel like Rosencrantz or Guildenstern: Stoppard's two characters don't know who they were, and spend a good deal of the play trying to work out who is who. A useful tip to help you do a PhD without going mad, is to write down what you want to do, and why. Also, note any early questions and sub questions. Then, when you start losing direction, you have something concrete to guide you and sharpen your focus. Of course, it might not always be enough to pick up a notebook and pen and write down (or reread) what your goal and motivation is. You may have descended into such a pit of despair that this doesn't help; you may be questioning *everything*; you may not know whether you're Rosencrantz or Guildenstern.

If this is the case, then it's time to go for a walk. Do anything to remind yourself that you're a physical being. Have a walk; a swim; a session at the gym. Do a supermarket shop (isn't your hunger and need to eat evidence of your corporality?). Bagpuss creator Oliver Postgate, speaking on Radio 4's *Desert Island Discs* (15 July 2007) talked about the need to always be doing something, in order to know that he exists. The very fact that you're doing a PhD, completing research, writing, producing a thesis, is a confirmation that you exist, that you are alive. So above all, don't waste time wondering whether you exist. Aren't questions about the reality and purpose of our existence themselves pointless? Alexander McCall Smith ponders this, via the character of Matthew, in one of the instalments of his daily novel in his *44 Scotland Street* series:

> Would [Matthew] be doing this for the rest of his life – sitting here, waiting for something to happen? And if that was all there was to it, then what exactly was the point? The

artists whose work he sold were at least making things, leaving something behind them, a corpus of work. He, by contrast, would make nothing, would leave nothing behind.

But was that not the fate of so many of us? ... [other] people might equally well look at their lives and ask what the point was.

Or should one really not ask that question, simply because the question in itself was a pointless one? Perhaps there was no real point to our existence – or none that we could discern – and that meant that the real question that had to be asked was this: How can I make my life bearable? We are here whether we like it or not, and by and large we seem to have a need to continue. In that case, the real question to be addressed is: How are we going to make the experience of being here as fulfilling, as good as possible? That is what Matthew thought.

(McCall Smith, 2007, p. 42)

If doing a PhD is something you really want to do, then hold on to that ambition, and know that you are producing something, you are making a contribution, no matter how small it might seem.

Post-modernism and the Holocaust

It is all well and good debating the existence of 'truth', but when it came to my topic of research – teaching the Holocaust – questions of historical evidence and truth are not debating points: they are fundamental. 'Holocaust deniers' claim that the Holocaust never happened and that the Jews invented it. Deniers dispute the historical details of the Holocaust, such as the operation of the gas chambers and the number of Jews killed, in order to claim that there was no Nazi policy to exterminate Jews during the Second World War. R.J. Evans discusses the challenge that the Holocaust presents to post-modernism (1997, pp. 124–5). He comments that 'post-modernist hyper-relativism' claims that history is incapable of establishing any real facts about the past, views historical documents as 'texts', the facts in them as 'rhetoric', and the historical accounts based on them as 'literature'; Evans suggests that this approach supports revisionist claims of Holocaust denial.

But the historical evidence of the Holocaust is the whole argument against deniers' false claims. The Holocaust happened. Post-modernist claims about the nature of history seemed to trivialize mass murder. The post-modernist theorist Haydn White is among those who have revised their position. According to White, he had been concerned in his earlier work to draw attention to the fact that historians did not simply write up their findings in a 'report' style, but used literary methods to 'construct' what they were writing, and such methods inevitably brought a 'fictive' element to their work. White's later work drew a sharper distinction between fiction and history (Evans, 1997, pp. 124–5).

Keeping your politics and prejudices out of your writing

As researchers, we attempt to get as close to the 'truth' as possible. Marwick has said that historians should try and keep themselves out of their writing, and so it is with researchers too. But this is easier said than done, as Gash's and Thompson's contrasting accounts of the Peterloo Massacre show. No matter how much your reading of philosophy makes you question your existence throughout your PhD research, you are human. And so it is very difficult to write with complete detachment. Like Gash and Thompson, the researcher brings something of themselves to their research because of *who* they are. To some extent, everyone's thesis is autobiographical. It is personal. You choose the field of study and the research question. What motivated you? Who *you* are – your values and beliefs – will have influenced the research question you have chosen.

Traditionally, PhD theses are written in the third person, with the researcher apparently remote from the research in order to demonstrate the honesty and integrity of their work. However, it has become evident that research, in whatever field, is more dependent on *who* is looking, rather than *what* is being observed. The thing to do is be honest about who you are and what has motivated you. As Marwick notes, 'writers and teachers should always state their fundamental assumptions, and readers and students should always seek to find out what these are' (2001, p. 2). At the same time it is important to avoid being polemical. Everyone comes to their research with certain prejudices and convictions. In line with feminist methods of research, theses now often include an autobiographical statement, usually in the form of a chapter where the researcher 'situates' themselves in the research.

My decision to write such a chapter was a response to E.H. Carr's maxim: study the historian before studying their work. He said that all historians have 'bees in their bonnets', and if you cannot detect the buzzing as you read their work then there was something wrong (Carr, 1961, p. 23). It may be that as researchers we cannot be completely objective in our research, but we should be as honest as possible. A biographical statement casts light on who you are and what angle you are coming at your research from, which is useful to the reader, as well as to yourself. (As noted above, it is certainly helpful to have a personal statement positioning yourself and your work in order to save your own sanity!) I used my introductory chapter to do this, and actually used the line, 'as a young, white, female, history teacher, what prompted me to design and undertake this research?'

Perhaps that line should have read: '... a young, white, female, Roman Catholic, history teacher ...'. I'm not sure why, at the time, I didn't note my religious belief. Perhaps I was being overly concerned about not wishing to cause offence, or to be accused of anti-Semitism. The Catholic Church has, historically, had a difficult relationship with Judaism, and anti-Semitism has its roots in religion. Early Christians blamed the Jews for the death of Christ; during the Middle Ages it was an unquestioned part of Christian doctrine that the Jews were guilty of the death of Christ. Crusaders passing through France and Germany, intending to 'rescue' the holy places of Christianity from the Arabs, slaughtered Jews on their way (Bresheeth, Hood and Jansz, 2000, pp. 6–7).

Relations between the Catholic Church and Judaism have improved since the Second Vatican Council. Christianity is about love, justice, peace and freedom. Perhaps subconsciously I avoided referring to my Catholicism because I didn't want readers to make assumptions or associations which were not accurate. The main aim of my work was to encourage debate about *how* the topic of the Holocaust should be approached in school history teaching, in order to improve classroom practice. Maybe I did not note my religious belief because I did not see it as relevant to that aim, and I did not want readers to be distracted by my faith.

In your writing, you must decide what is relevant. What biographical details do you think it is important to include? Will you leave anything out? This may be a conscious or unconscious decision. Was it necessary for me to note that I was female? It is a label that Judith Butler would claim to be redundant. In her book *Gender Trouble* (1990) she argues that identity is an illusion created by our performances. Gender, she says, is a performance: it's what you *do* at particular times rather than a universal *who you are*.

Undercover research

Identity is an interesting area, which is also related to undercover research. The issue of 'truth' is not only relevant to how you write up your research; it is also relevant to how you conduct it. The journalist Donal MacIntyre has won awards for his work as an undercover reporter. In MacIntyre's book about the experience of living four undercover lives, he raises several issues relevant to the academic researcher who might decide to work in a similar way – assuming a particular personality in order to become part of the group they want to research. I know of those who do this sort of undercover research. For reasons of security MacIntyre cannot publicly name and thank all those who have helped him in his acknowledgements. And because it would be inappropriate to 'blow their cover', I cannot name friends who have worked or are working 'undercover' in their fields. This kind of approach can seem appealing. It avoids the 'Hawthorne Effect', where people being observed during a research study change their behaviour because they know they are being watched (for more on the Hawthorne Effect see Parsons (1974)). MacIntyre writes:

> Traditional journalistic methods don't always deliver the true and accurate picture – undiluted and unadulterated – of who and what people are. Only by seeing people speaking and operating among their own is it possible to get an accurate sense of what they're about in true documentary fashion. Undercover reporting can be the purest form of documentary – the definitive 'fly-on-the-wall'.
>
> (MacIntyre, 1999, pp. 9–10)

And so it is with social research. But there are dangers: the researcher must be careful not to influence their research:

> The golden rule is this: as an undercover reporter, you must never encourage anyone to do or say anything that they would not otherwise do if you had not been there ... The essence of the technique is getting people to tell their stories in their own words, as they would to one of their own. But this could only happen if they believe I am who I say I am, be it football hooligan, care worker, bodyguard or fashion photographer.
>
> (MacIntyre, 1999, p. 8)

There are ethical questions here, related to 'truth', about honesty and trust. This approach is very much more involved than observation. You have to assume a different identity (you are no longer your 'true' self). Not only do you take on a different personality, but you may also find you leave something of yourself behind when you leave your field of study.

> In the course of a day I have assumed four different personalities, worn four different wardrobes and spoken four different street dialects, and left a little bit of me behind in each of those worlds.
>
> (MacIntyre, 1999, p. 7)

You need to think carefully about this approach to your research. If you want to return to your field of study to do more work, you can't reveal yourself. When MacIntyre revealed himself to be an undercover reporter after playing 'Tony', a bouncer doorman and petty criminal, for 11 months, he succeeded in befriending a Ferrari-driving drug dealer called Wayne. He ended up in jail. The programme's evidence led to investigations by three police forces and won two Royal Television Society journalism awards. It also earned me three death threats and a £50,000 price on my head. I had to leave the country after it was broadcast.

(MacIntyre, 1999, p. 9)

Clearly, due consideration needs to be given to your own personal safety before embarking on undercover research. MacIntyre also notes the importance of ethical practice: 'The strict guidelines within broadcasting organizations about covert filming mean that, every time I go into the field, a BBC committee or compliance officer has to grant me permission first' (MacIntyre, 1999, p. 8).

There are psychological pressures associated with working in this way, which MacIntyre is acutely aware of. He is a sociology graduate, and interestingly he invited Professor Howard Tumber of City University and Professor Craig Mahoney of Wolverhampton University to undertake sociological studies on the psychological pressures of working undercover, and co-operated with them fully during the production of his 1999 series *MacIntyre Undercover* for the BBC.

The truth is out there

I do not believe that we as human beings can always know or 'get to' the truth. But I do believe it exists, and this position is informed by my belief in God. In a sense I have a 'Big Brother' view of God. This does not mean that I believe God is a voyeur who watches us and is entertained by our activities, or that I believe God sets us 'tasks' for his amusement. I don't think life is like a game show, or that St Peter has a Geordie accent. But I believe God is omnipotent, omnipresent and omniscient: God has infinite awareness, understanding and insight. Only God possesses complete knowledge. For us, getting at the truth is more difficult. We are not completely objective, or in full possession of the facts.

In February 2007 BBC2 screened *The Verdict*, a fictitious

rape trial of an 'internationally famous footballer', Damien Scott, and his friend, James Greer. The alleged 'victim', Anna Crane, claimed to have been raped by Scott, Greer and a third unknown man after she met the footballer in a hotel bar during a night out in London with her friend, Clare Golding. Both of these women, the 'defendants' and the 'witnesses' were played by actors in an unscripted trial which took place in a real courtroom, with recently retired judge Lord Neil Dennison presiding, and three of the UK's leading criminal barristers: Joanna Greenberg QC, Jane Humphryes QC and George Carter-Stephenson QC. A celebrity jury delivered the verdict. 'The truth is what you choose to believe', ran the line trailing the programme. It made for fascinating viewing, allowing viewers to see how the criminal courts work and throwing up all kinds of issues about juries, and how we attempt to discover the truth.

The jury could not convict Greer and Scott on the basis of the evidence presented, and acquitted both men, but with serious misgivings. Barrister Joanna Greenberg commented following their verdict, 'If you ask me whether justice has been done, well, applying the strict burden and standard of proof, it probably has been. But has Anna Crane received justice? Probably not' ('The Verdict', 2007). The actors who played the characters involved with the case had met before the trial and taken part in an unscripted improvisation. The trial treated the events of that night as if they were real. So just as in a real trial, the viewer was left at the end of the programme not knowing whether justice had been done or not. Ingrid Tarrant was a member of the jury: 'I will live with this wondering – was I right, was I wrong? Were we right, were we wrong?' Without a script, or a recording of the event, the truth about the improvization that took place is not known to anyone but the actors involved. But, although we do not know the truth, it does exist. Either the 'rape' took place, or it did not.

If I can't get at *the* truth, what's the point of my research?

So, where does all this leave your research? In truth(!), I found philosophy very interesting, but too much reading in this area left me feeling that my work had little value in the wider scheme of things. My own starting point had been my class-room experience. As I noted in Chapter One, the Holocaust is one of only four topics which must be taught in secondary school history to pupils aged 11 to 13. The other three topics are the two World Wars and the Cold War. Early drafts of the National Curriculum for History published in 2000 apparently included the Holocaust as the *only* compulsory content (Haydn, 2000, p. 135). Having experienced difficulty teaching about the Holocaust to 13 and 14 year olds, I wanted to find out why it had been included on the curriculum as a compulsory topic. Was the main purpose historical, or was it social or moral? I thought if I could find out why the topic had a special status on the History Curriculum, it would support colleagues in their teaching and consequently improve pupils' learning and understanding. At first I had thought I could find out 'the right way' to teach the Holocaust in school history. But I was naive to think I could come up with any definitive 'true' answers about how to teach this topic. What my research did was make a contribution to the existing body of research and encourage further debate on the issue. And it is the same within the sciences.

The general public seem to assume that science has 'all the answers'. It is a view that the media apparently support, and there is much attention given to 'what scientists say'. Take the following selection of news headlines: 'Middle Ages were warmer than today, say scientists' (the *Daily Telegraph*, 5 April 2003); 'Scientists "switch off" arthritis with new drug' (the *Daily Mail*, 14 July 2004); 'Magic mushrooms could help depression, say scientists' (the *Daily Mail*, 11 July 2006); 'Danger from radiation is exaggerated, say scientists' (*The Times*, 10 July 2006); 'Beautiful people tend to have girls, say scientists' (*The Times*, 30 July 2006); 'Teenagers can't help being selfish, say scientists' (the *Daily Mail*, 7 September 2006); 'The greater your weight, the lower your IQ, say scientists' (the *Daily Telegraph*, 6 October 2006); 'Scientists find the gene that can help you fidget yourself thin' (the *Daily Mail*, 6 June 2007).

If 'scientists say' something, then it must be true. In recent years there has been much discussion in the media about stem cell research, and its potential for curing a multitude of diseases. But Professor Robert Winston warned in September 2005 that 'the notion that a host of cures for serious, degenerative disorders are just around the corner is fanciful' (Amos, 2005, 9 September). According to the BBC report, Lord Winston said the potential benefits of this research had been oversold to the public, although he added that 'of course, the study of stem cells is one of the most exciting areas in biology but I think that it is unlikely that embryonic stem cells are likely to be useful in healthcare for a long time' (Amos, 2005, 9 September).

Giving such credence to scientific opinion reflects a 'positivist' viewpoint. Positivism is a philosophy which states that the only authentic knowledge is scientific knowledge, which can only be obtained from the verification of theories through scientific procedures. This theory was developed by Auguste Comte in the nineteenth century. The positivist view is often shared by those in government. Take this report – again from the *Daily Mail* (8 January 2007) – on organic food:

NO EVIDENCE ORGANIC FOOD IS BETTER FOR OUR HEALTH, SAYS MINISTER

Highly-priced organic food is no better for us than conventionally-grown farm produce, a Minister claimed.

Environment Secretary David Miliband said consumers who opted for chemical-free, naturally-produced food did so as a 'lifestyle choice' rather than because science had proved it was healthier.

The technocrats seem to share the view that scientific research can reveal 'the truth'. But is there only one 'truth'? There is a growing body of evidence that organic food is more nutritious. For example, studies have shown that organic milk contains more omega-3 fatty acids than non-organic milk (Dewhurst, Fisher, Tweed and Wilkins, 2003; Ellis et al., 2006). But in

December 2006 the *Daily Mail* ran a story under the headline 'Organic chicken "less nutritious" than battery-farmed birds' (3 December). This was based on research conducted by Dr Alistair Paterson of Strathclyde University (Jahan, Paterson and Spickett, 2006). The research contradicts earlier work which revealed organic chicken contained more omega-3, had less fat, and tasted better than conventionally reared chicken (Castellini, Mugnai and Dal Bosco, 2002). Within the scientific community, the debate continues. After all, 'the scientists' (who complete the experiments and write up the research) are human, they are not automatons.

There is a view that research happens in a remote place, an 'ivory tower'. When I hear that term I always imagine the story of Rapunzel. But unlike Rapunzel, scientists are not cut off from everyday life. The scientist chooses what aspects of their work to focus on; the size of their sample; and where their samples come from. And there is not only the issue of possible personal bias from the scientist researcher – whether intentional or unintentional – but also the question of who is funding the research. I am not debunking scientific research, but making the point that researchers in the sciences are no more or less independent or objective than those working in the humanities. Despite the great faith the media and the general public have in science, the question of 'truth' and objectivity in research is as relevant in the sciences as in any other field of research.

It is unlikely, therefore, that you will come up with any one, definitive 'truth' as a result of your PhD research. Sometimes, what you are doing may seem very small, but do try to appreciate it: what you are doing is adding something to the bigger picture. Dr David E. Simpson notes that, looking back, he felt he 'undervalued the work I did as I still had the illusion that science progressed through massive breakthroughs and intellectual revolutions'. Don't undervalue your own research. There may be occasional big breakthroughs and intellectual revolutions but on the whole, in every field, *research is about making a contribution to existing knowledge and debate*. This is what Professor David Bellamy sees as important about doing a PhD: 'It is how real knowledge progresses: hard work and discussion'.

I want to end this chapter with a reference to 'truth' from

The Last Confession by Roger Crane. First performed in 2007 and starring David Suchet, this play is about the circumstances surrounding the sudden death of Pope John Paul I, after just 33 days in office. The lead character, Cardinal Benelli, makes a comment in the play relevant to the PhD process and the pursuit of 'truth' in research. I'll leave you with this:

> Truth ... Pope Paul believed that truth is found only through suffering.
>
> (Crane, 2007, p. 30)

Chapter Six

Which came first, the chicken or the egg?

I walked past a stand of greetings cards one morning. There was one in particular which stood out. It said, 'Where there's cake, there's hope.' It's true! I always bake for the Saturday School sessions I teach at Goldsmiths. I think food plays an important role in the PhD experience. There is little I find more comforting than a cup of tea and a piece of cake. And I find the process of baking very therapeutic. My husband always knew when things weren't going well – he would come home to find wire cooling racks full of cakes and biscuits. But when I needed more immediate gratification, there were jelly babies. I was never a sweet eater before I began my PhD. But after one tutorial – during which the discussion between myself and my supervisor focused on my methodology chapter – I remember sitting at the train station and eating an entire bag of jelly babies. It is the only time I have ever eaten a whole bag of sweets. It helped.

I got through quite a few jelly babies while writing my thesis. I also found dolly mixtures a comfort while trying to write a difficult chapter, or staring at a blank computer screen. I don't think I am alone in this regard. It might not be jelly babies for you, but if you don't already have one you will probably discover your own particular favourite while writing your thesis. After I made my confession in an article for the *Independent* my experience was endorsed: 'Just read your article recommending jelly babies for thesis writing, sound advice!' (Dr David E. Simpson). 'I never tried jelly babies, but I must have consumed several hundred Jaffa cakes during the last three-and-a-bit-years' (Dr Alex Cousins). The photographer who came from the newspaper to take my picture for the article told me about her sister's experience of completing a PhD in archaeology: she ate *a lot* of Ferrero Rocher chocolates.

When *do* you write your methodology chapter?

Statistics collected during the Great Exhibition in 1851 showed that 1,092,337 bottles of soft drink, 934,691 bath buns and 28,046 sausage rolls were among the refreshments sold and consumed. It would have been interesting to have kept a similar count of the confectionery I consumed during the writing of my thesis – the methodology chapter in particular. Exactly how many dolly mixtures did I eat? I found this chapter ridiculously difficult to write, not least because my two supervisors had conflicting views about when to write it. One told me the methodology should be written before anything else. The other believed it was best left until later, and written in retrospect. Do you write the methodology as a 'map' to follow, or do you complete your journey first and then make a drawing of where you have been? Which came first, the chicken or the egg? I tended towards the view of my lead supervisor, who said 'Write the methodology at the end.' Much easier to write about how the chick had grown up, rather than to predict the likely future of the egg.

Charles Campbell notes that when he started writing up his thesis he

> didn't start at the beginning, but dived in with the results chapters and conclusion – I only returned to the introduction at the end, when I was 100 per cent sure what I was introducing.

This is an issue linked to writing up your thesis (discussed in Chapter Three), so that you don't leave 'hostages to fortune' (Chapter Nine). The methodology chapter underpins the thesis; it is the foundation upon which the rest of the thesis is built, so it needs to be laid down well. Although you may be more interested in your findings, the examiners will be just as interested – if not more so – in how you organized and completed your study. Remember, you get your PhD in large part for showing that you are capable of designing and completing research. You do also have to demonstrate originality and produce a piece of writing worthy of publication, but don't forget that a PhD is a professional qualification.

As it turned out, both of my supervisors were right: there were parts of my methodology chapter – for example, the section about the development of history as a discipline – which could be written before my research was complete, and which would help me position myself in the research. Writing a section on the 'history of history' involved reading and synthesizing the work of others. But there were also sections of my methodology which were much easier to write in retrospect: how I went about my study; what methods I chose to use, and why; and the issues which were raised during my study. This last point is important: the methodology chapter is an opportunity to pre-empt questions which may come up during the viva. Not everyone will agree with what you have written, but as long as your research is rigorous, it doesn't matter if your examiners don't actually like your conclusions.

Research methods

You should be trained in both quantitative and qualitative methods at your university when you begin your PhD. These courses will explain, and guide you through, the many and various research methods you can choose to research your PhD, and their respective values and limitations. There are also numerous books available on the subject. My own PhD drew on historical research and interviews, the latter having become 'one of the major tools of social research' (Hitchcock and Hughes, 1995, p. 153), so I have devoted all of Chapter Seven to interviews: arranging them; conducting them; and transcribing them.

I hated writing about my methodology; I found it very laborious and not a little dull. I had wanted my thesis to be readable, but found it difficult to write about which methods I had selected, and compare their pros and cons, in an interesting way. I used to think: 'Couldn't the examiners take this as read?' Surely much of what I was writing was a repetition of what they had read so many times before in PhD theses, for example that oral history is valuable because it is a first-hand account, but limited because memory is fallible ... The first part of my PhD traced the development of the Holocaust as a topic on the National Curriculum for History, so I drew on a number of documents. It was like GCSE history all over again: the use of documents, like the use of any method, presents a number of issues which had to be highlighted in my methodology chapter.

It was frustrating because I was sure that the examiners – and anyone else reading my thesis – would themselves be aware of the issues, but of course the point is that the readers need to be sure that *I* was aware of the issues. So I wrote a bit about newspapers. Newspaper reports not only provide a chronicle of events, but attempt to shape the reader's perception of them. Reports may reflect the opinion of the journalist, or express the political view of the editor or owner of the newspaper. It is important to remember that all newspapers present contemporary events from a particular ideological viewpoint. Arthur Marwick writes, 'these sources are very rich for attitudes, assumptions, mentalities, and values' (Marwick, 2001, p. 168), but they cannot be taken on trust.

One of my most important sources was the History Working Group minutes so my methodology chapter also needed to refer to minutes: I know from school staff meetings that secretaries can be instructed not to minute an item, or to word it carefully. Minutes are not necessarily a true or complete record of all that was discussed in a meeting, as Marwick also notes: 'Minutes, reports of meetings, and so on, recording what a body as a whole *agreed* its decisions to be, can be incomplete and slanted' (Marwick, 2001, p. 166). I had read in the late Professor Robert Phillips' book about the development of the National Curriculum for History that one of the group members he had interviewed alluded to a 'slim majority' which resulted in the absence of the Second World War as a specific study unit in the Interim Report (R. Phillips, 1998a, p. 80). This was an extremely interesting and exciting point from my perspective, but the minutes of that particular meeting do not reveal a debate or a vote on the issue. Who were the 'slim majority'? How forcefully did the minority disagree? What were the arguments? I would have to use other sources to try and get some answers.

In the first part of my thesis, I also drew on the memoirs of political figures. Autobiography as a genre is interesting. Like the identity of the self, a life story is a construction. Politicians write their memoirs for a purpose: to provide their own account of their life and career; to defend, explain or 'put on record' their actions in government. The authors of these accounts usually write some time after the events being described, using diaries and notes from their period in office. Therefore certain additions can be made with the benefit of hindsight. A quotation from Margaret Thatcher's *The Downing Street Years* comes to mind. Concluding her writing on the National Curriculum, Thatcher writes: 'By the time I left office I was convinced that there would have to be a new drive to simplify the National Curriculum and testing' (Thatcher, 1993, p. 597). This may be true, but when Thatcher wrote that in the first volume of her memoirs, published in October 1993, she may well have been aware of the previous announcement in

April 1993 about the Dearing Review, which was set up to review the National Curriculum.

In 2007 there was some discussion surrounding the publication of Alastair Campbell's diary. He made it clear at the time of publication – and this was widely commented upon – that he had edited the diaries, provoking comments such as these:

> A penetrating insight into a fascinating period of government, or the latest bit of spin from a Blairite propagandist trying to rewrite history?

> Alastair Campbell's diaries have already attracted both descriptions. Perhaps worse, however, is the widespread criticism that the 800-page work has a yawning Gordon Brown-sized black hole at the centre of it.

> Mr Campbell has been happy to confirm that he left out big chunks about the relationship between the current and former prime ministers, for the simple reason he didn't want to hand David Cameron ammunition – thereby confirming that these 'lost' episodes would be damaging to the Labour government.
>
> (Assinder, 2007, 9 July)

Memoirs are a no more or less perfect account than any other historical source, but they are interesting in themselves.

I also used questionnaires, which were sent to teachers and designed to gain some basic information and a snapshot of their views. The idea was that the questionnaires would be used as the basis for a follow-up interview. I distributed 40 multiple-choice questionnaires to history teachers at 20 schools, and I tried to contact two members of each department in order to gauge how clear objectives were within the same department. My sample included a variety of schools: grammar, secondary modern, faith-based, and independent. I included stamped self-addressed envelopes and an A4 flyer explaining the purpose of my research, in order to make it easy for teachers to take part in my research. But I only received nine returns over the next two months. Disappointed, I talked to one of my supervisors over coffee one morning. How were things going? Not as well as I had hoped. He suggested sending out a follow-up letter, explaining that I had received a number of replies, and that there was still time for colleagues to take part in my survey. I didn't want my recipients to think things weren't going well! The follow-up letter resulted in another six returns. Time was pressing, and this would have to be good enough.

I started contacting teachers as soon as I received their replies, but this was proving tricky too. I wasn't surprised − it wasn't long since I'd been teaching full-time myself, and I knew the demands on a teacher's time. It was necessary to make several telephone calls, sometimes over two or three weeks, to the teachers' schools. And when contact *was* made, the inevitable school trips or forthcoming Ofsted inspections − to say nothing of heavy workloads − meant interviews were difficult to arrange. So, despite my having 15 questionnaire returns, I could only interview ten teachers. This took longer than I'd antici-pated: four months. But despite the size of the sample, the data gathered assisted my reflection on the teaching of the Holocaust in school history, and resulted in an interesting and important chapter of my thesis.

At one point, I considered extending my study and exploring what pupils thought was important about the topic of the Holocaust. For that, I would have used 'focus groups'. In recent years focus groups have apparently been used by New Labour to keep a finger on the pulse of Middle England; such groups are also commonly used in business. As with any method of research there are pros and cons, but focus groups are quick and cheap to organize, and suitable for eliciting data from children − although they may be shy at the beginning of a session. If I had gone ahead with this part of my research I would have con-ducted the focus groups in the schools (a familiar and safe setting in which the children will be comfortable), during a single lesson (usually 50 minutes to an hour in secondary schools). I would have planned an activity related to what I wanted to discover, which could then be used as the basis for a group discussion. With adults such a discussion can be started with a question or statement, but children may 'clam up'.

I had clear plans for proceeding: I would have gone into the schools and got the children together in groups of six to eight, with the help of their teachers. To ensure that the children were at ease, I would have organized friendship groups or single-sex groups. I would have explained who I was and what, in general terms, I was doing. (I didn't want to pre-empt the outcome or influence the research: children are often eager to please, and may give you the response they think you want, rather than their own reactions and opinions).

I would have worn my 'PhD uniform' of smart casual wear rather than my 'teacher's uniform', a trouser suit. As I wrote in Chapter Four, clothes have a language of their own and send out a particular message, and I would not want the children to identify me as another teacher: I would have wanted enough authority to conduct the focus group, but not so much that the pupils might hold back their views, or worry that I would report their comments back to their teachers. Drawing on my teaching experience, I would stress the need to use short, to-the-point questions. Interview questions can be rather rambling. But a focus group is not an interview; it should be an interesting conversation, and children – indeed any participants who are not engaged with the subject matter, as you are – will not respond to unfocused questions. You need to make sure your participants know what you are asking them.

If you run a focus group, I suggest you make a plan of where participants are sitting, so that you can use their names. This means you can direct questions at those who have said less (there may be one or two who dominate the conversation – one of the drawbacks of such groups). Once you know participants' names and voices, you will find the discussion easier to transcribe. There is an issue about giving rewards or incentives to those involved in your research, though it is a feature of psychological research, for example. Personally, I would thank the children at the end, and give them some sweets (as you see, confectionery plays a big part in the PhD experience!).

There is no danger of the research being skewed if rewards are given at the end. You might also want to think about how to encourage other participants to take part in your research. Perhaps if I had offered something to my teachers I would have received more questionnaire replies. I did include a nice gel pen with the questionnaires – charities often send a pen with direct debit forms and leaflets about their work, don't they? It's a clever idea: a free gift with their logo on, and a guarantee that you have everything you need to hand when you read their literature and (they hope) decide you want to make a contribution! (I did receive a book of first class stamps once, with a letter from a researcher doing some work for the Office for National Statistics. She planned to call at my house, hoping I would give her a short interview about her research topic – family resources, I think. At the time I was moving, and busy renovating the house but not actually living in it. She never did call ... I was very pleased with the stamps though: very useful for the 'new address' cards).

Pre-empting issues

Just as the literature review isn't just about books, because it includes other forms of media – newspapers, television, radio – the methodology chapter isn't just about what you did and why.

I was particularly concerned not to cause offence in my thesis. Research involving sensitive issues like the Holocaust is closely scrutinized, and fraught with accusations of anti-Semitism. Like the British Empire, this area of historical study has become highly politicized. This issue concerned me, and when I discussed it with one of my supervisors he told me about a Radio 4 programme in which Linda Colley's book, *Captives*, was discussed. I listened to the programme, which raised a number of relevant issues I decided to discuss in my thesis. Here is an excerpt from my methodology chapter:

> Marwick (2001) makes clear that when writing history, language must be explicit and precise so as to reduce misunderstandings and misrepresentations. I endeavour in this thesis to be clear and exact, though historians can still encounter criticism when they challenge taken-for-granted assumptions. Take for example Linda Colley's book *Captives*, in which she details the experience of 'hundreds of thousands of English, Welsh, Scottish and Irish men, women and children who were taken captive in different regions of the

extra-European world during the first quarter millennium of British imperial enterprise' (Colley, 2002, p.3). The majority of these people, she says, were 'insignificant'. 'They were soldiers, minor traders, sailors, camp followers, various womenfolk and children' (Colley, 2002, 17 October) whose experience as captives and as slaves (in North Africa) provides a very different perspective on empire than is traditionally understood. Colley attempts to undertake 'a work both of individual recovery and imperial revision' (Colley, 2002, p. xvii). She has produced a history of people who were also victims of Britain's empire-building.

But despite noting in her acknowledgements that 'I have been constantly reminded while writing *Captives* – and have sought throughout to make clear – that other, very different stories exist about the empire that the British once made' (Colley, 2002, p. xvii), and making clear in her introduction her actual motivation, Colley's work was challenged by Professor Catherine Hall during BBC Radio 4's *In Our Time* in October 2002. Hall felt that Colley's work might undermine the suffering of black people enslaved and oppressed by the British Empire. Hall's defence of black slaves is similar to Deborah Lipstadt's defence of the memory of the Holocaust and its victims, which is discussed in the following chapter. Research involving sensitive issues including the Empire and the Holocaust is closely scrutinized, and fraught with accusations of racism and anti-Semitism; both areas have become highly politicized. Work like Colley's is important if we want to understand the full historical picture. Interestingly, it was Hall and not Colley who raised the issue of comparative suffering:

'I would want to put that [Colley's] picture of white vulnerability and white insecurity which we are getting from the stories of those captured in India, or Britons in North America, or in North Africa, against other people's insecurities and vulnerabilities in the Empire over this period. So okay, hundreds of thousands of Britons were captured in war. But their status as captives of war was different from the

status for example of those who were enslaved, a very dif-
ferent situation to be a slave from being a captive.'
(Catherine Hall, in the BBC Radio 4 programme
In Our Time, 17 October 2002)

Hall spelled out her point: 'Each individual story is worth
telling. But what the implications of these stories are in terms
of rethinking histories of empire might be something of a
different matter.'

Felipe Fernandez-Armesto defended Colley's work:
'It doesn't take anything away from the plight of black slaves
to say that white people were also enslaved and were in a
sense captives of their own empires because I think Linda has
done a great service by reminding us that one of the things
which makes empire wicked and evil is its effects on the
imperial master as well as the victims.'
(Felipe Fernandez-Armesto in the BBC Radio 4 Programme
In Our Time, 17 October 2002)

Melvyn Bragg ended the programme by asking the panel:
'Do you think that the received perception of slavery and its
associations increasingly solely with the British has coloured
our view of empire so much that it has made it extremely
difficult to talk about the British Empire over the last 30 to
40 years? Has it become too awful and too massive to assess
and tackle imperial studies?'

Colley's response was particularly relevant to this thesis:
'I think empire is like war. It is a recurrent human practice,
indeed it's still with us in various forms. While we may hate
war – we should hate war – we still want to study it, we need
to study it, and the same applies to empire. It's difficult, it's
often horrible, it's deeply contentious as this programme has
shown, but that is precisely why we need to look at it more.'
(Linda Colley in the BBC Radio 4 Programme *In Our Time*,
17 October 2002)

Given that this thesis is unlikely to resolve the issue of what
history teachers' objectives should be, my main aim is to
encourage debate about *how* the topic of the Holocaust

should be approached in school history. It is a debate which is difficult to tackle given the enormity and complexity of the Holocaust; but it is an important debate which it would seem needs to be looked at. Given the above example, I see no harm in having reiterated a principal aim of this study here, in addition to highlighting a major pitfall in conducting work which involves sensitive issues.

(L. Russell, 2005, pp. 82–4)

What is interesting about this excerpt is that while one super-visor thought it very good, the other did not think it should be included in the thesis. There are issues here about how to communicate well with more than one supervisor. Whose advice to follow? Ultimately it was my choice. I thought the section was important, and one of the most interesting parts of my methodology chapter, so I included it. I was glad I did! At my viva, the external examiner commented on this passage, saying that she particularly liked it. Both my internal and external examiners asked for copies of my thesis, and the external examiner wanted to use the methodology chapter as a model with her PhD students!

What issues are relevant to your study?

Someone I spoke to in the course of my research had written a good deal in her own methodology chapter about the import-ance of making clear to interviewees the basis on which an interview is conducted. Is it just for information? Will it be written up word for word? Will it be published? Can the interviewee be granted anonymity? This woman was on one of the bodies which reviewed the National Curriculum for His-tory. I wanted to talk to her about the work of that group, and I contacted her:

'What exactly do you want?'

'To find out more about how you conduct interviews.'

'You mean interviewing to gain information?'

'Er, yes.'

I thought about this. Weren't all interviews for gaining information? The way I had been running my interviews was to take notes verbatim, write up the interviews word for word, and then check transcripts with the interviewees to confirm their accuracy.

And that's just what I did in this instance. But when it came to emailing the transcript to check it with the interviewee, things got a bit sticky. I received an email from her expressing astonishment, and asking me to rewrite my notes more appropriately and to destroy the original transcript. I hold my hands up. I hadn't written up the meeting appropriately. The interviewee had been very candid in the interview because I had said that what I wanted was *information*. The transcript, although accurate, made it look like a formal interview from which I was prepared to quote freely. In fact, I wouldn't have quoted anything without her permission, but she didn't know that.

I would advise you not to destroy any written material you produce (including drafts of your thesis – you may want to refer back to earlier drafts of chapters). Put a line through it with a note saying why you decided not to use it. File it at the back of your filing cabinet. But don't shred it or bin it. Perhaps it is because I have a history background, but I find it difficult to destroy documents. They may be relevant later, and transcripts and drafts are part of the historical record of a PhD. Also, for the sake of my own reputation, and to help me obtain future interviews, I would always seek permission to use quotations from individuals I wanted to name in my research.

When the late Princess of Wales cooperated with Andrew Morton for a book about her story, he was asked not to make known her involvement during her lifetime. He kept to his word, but following her death he revealed that she had in fact been the source of the original book, and published a second edition: *Diana: Her True Story – In Her Own Words* (Morton, 1998). It is relevant that it was the Princess herself, and not others close to her, who was the source for this book. It tells us something about the position the Princess felt she was in at the time. Morton kept the drafts of the chapters of his book which had been checked and annotated by the Princess. This material has now become part of the historical record.

Researchers always know more than they can tell. Even if you can't write about something at the time, your knowledge is good 'for information': your understanding of the background helps to inform you, and assist your writing generally. And there may come a point when you can reveal more. Undoubtedly there will be more from Alastair Campbell about Blair and Brown, in the fullness of time.

Chapter Seven

Quiche and boiled cabbage

I've had lunch with many of my interviewees. The most memorable menu was quiche and cabbage – the latter boiled for exactly 20 minutes! The most memorable venue promised to be Rockingham Castle, though when I went to interview Commander Saunders Watson – whose family owns the castle – he had moved to another house on the estate. His son had taken over the running of the castle. Nevertheless it was a lovely lunch, and when the Commander drove me back to the train station, we did pop into the castle, and I was given a guidebook.

Writing letters

The first point of contact with those you wish to interview is usually a letter. How do you entice the recipient to take part in your research? I remember being very concerned about letter-writing. At first I asked my supervisors to read the letters I wrote before I sent them. I met Professor Victor Newman by chance on the train to London while I was writing this book, and in the course of our conversation we talked about writing letters to 'elites' – people in positions of power or authority. 'You've got to make your project sound sexy,' he said. It's true. But I never found much in the way of guidance on how to write 'request letters'. I guess it's assumed that a researcher would know how to write a letter – true enough, but this is really about *crafting* a letter: explaining briefly who you are; briefly outlining what your research is about and why it is important; establishing some credibility; flattering your reader's ego; and saying what you want from him/her. And all on one side of A4! Would you bother to turn the page, if you got a letter from someone you didn't know? We live in an age of media soundbites: people are used to getting information instantly, and your interviewees are likely to be busy people, so you must make it easy for them to give you what you want.

To establish my credibility I used university headed notepaper for my letters, and always mentioned my supervisors. The responses to the letters I sent out during my PhD research, asking for interviews with key players in the formation of the National Curriculum for History, were positive. I did have to write a second letter to the Chair of the History Working Group, who told me later that he always refused the first request for an interview, to test whether the writer was really interested, and keen to arrange a meeting. When I made a second request, he agreed to be interviewed.

Organizing a meeting

I always travelled to meet my interviewees, and often met them in their own homes. Several meetings took place on neutral ground at the Royal Festival Hall. I love the South Bank, and it was easy for me to walk there from Charing Cross. It seemed to suit the people I met, too. The only difficulty is that it is easy to miss people there. (As a child I remember waiting for friends with my family for about an hour – they had been there all the time, just around the corner!) So I always suggested a specific place to meet, such as the ticket hall, or outside the bookshop. Meeting is especially difficult when you don't know what the other person looks like. One day I waited outside the bookshop for over an hour – the person I was waiting for was 100 yards away, looking at the river! Perhaps we should have both been carrying a carnation. Anyway, that was a few years ago. Today's ubiquitous mobile phones should prevent such disappointments.

Interview issues

When I wrote to Professor John Roberts to ask if he would be interviewed by me about his role on the History Working Group, he replied that he would, but that I was 'of course, turning to oral evidence – of all historical sources, in my view the least reliable!' According to John Tosh such scepticism regarding oral evidence is not uncommon within the historical profession (Tosh, 1991, p. 207). As with all methods of research there are issues about the conduct of interviews. Tosh explains: 'In an interview each party is affected by the other. It is the historian who selects the informant and indicates the area of interest.' He adds: 'The presence of an outsider affects the atmosphere in which the informant recalls the past and talks about it' (1991, p. 213). Tosh also highlights the limitations of personal memory:

> Memories, however precise and vivid, are filtered through subsequent experience. They may be contaminated by what has been absorbed from other sources (especially the media); they may be overlaid by nostalgia ('times were good then'), or distorted by a sense of grievance about deprivation in childhood which only took root in later life.
>
> (Tosh, 1991, p. 213)

Interviewees may also have forgotten something which the historian would find useful. In some cases, however, questions might prompt interviewees' recollections. Dr Trude Levi is a Hungarian Jew who has given many talks in England and Germany about her experiences during the Holocaust. In her book *Did you ever meet Hitler, Miss?* she touches on the issue of memory:

> We were only once taken out of Birkenau-B2 camp during our time there, when we were sent out for a bath and given clean clothing. I had forgotten the incident completely until someone asked me one day whether any of the guards had ever hit me. Then it came back to me; we were walking barefoot over extremely sharp stones on our way to the bath. One of the stones rolled over and I slipped out of the line. The next second, I was lying on the ground. One of the guards hit me so hard on the nape of the neck that I had blacked out for a moment and lost my balance. I managed to get up and get back into the line before they could hit me again. Because I was concentrating so hard on where to tread I remember very little else about the incident, where we

were going or what the surroundings were like. But I do remember this was the only time we left the camp.

(Levi, 2003, p. 16)

It is important to bear in mind when you're conducting interviews: not only is memory fallible, but interviewees (like politicians in their memoirs) may offer a particular version of events portraying their own actions in a certain light. While this may be interesting in itself, accuracy requires some corroborative evidence: 'Oral evidence, like all verbal materials, requires critical evaluation deployed in conjunction with all the other available sources' (Tosh, 1991, p. 215).

As noted in the previous chapter, interviews are 'one of the major tools of social research' (Hitchcock and Hughes, 1995, p. 153). Extensive use of this technique of data collection across the social sciences and in educational research has resulted in enormous diversity in the form and styles of interviews that have developed. Hitchcock and Hughes (1995) point to a range of interview types, including 'standardized' interviews, encompassing 'structured' or 'survey' interviews; 'semi-structured' interviews; and group interviews which are either structured or semi-structured. In a structured interview questions are usually closed rather than open, and are asked in the same order to each interviewee. This assumes that there is such a thing as 'objective truth' (something which we can be less certain about, in light of the previous chapter). Critics of this approach, such as Elliot Mishler, have described structured interviews as 'systematic and hierarchical' because 'interviewers initiate topics, direct the flow of talk, decide when a response is adequate, and only interviewees disclose their views' (Mishler, 1990, p. 30).

'Non-standardized' interviews include 'ethnographic'; 'unstructured group'; 'oral'; 'life history'; and informal interviews, as well as conversations and eavesdropping. Unlike a structured interview, the semi-structured interview is flexible, and for this reason 'tends to be the most favoured by educational researchers' (Hitchcock and Hughes, 1995, p. 157). This form of interview allows researchers to use a list of key questions as prompts rather than as a fixed framework. The same key questions are asked each time but can be reordered by the interviewer, who is able to 'probe' and encourage respondents to expand on their answers. Because I often conducted interviews in interviewees' own homes, and because I was asking about their memories, opinions and professional documents, I considered that my interviewees held the balance of power. I therefore needed to develop a rapport with them and gain their trust, if I was to elicit from them the richest possible data. Lofland (1971) points to the importance of the interviewer familiarizing themselves with the biographical and contextual features of their interviewee's history, background and outlook. Prior to conducting interviews I researched individuals, for example reading any articles and books which they had published, and learning about their lives and careers.

I wanted my interviewees to feel as though they were engaged in an interesting conversation rather than being interviewed. I sometimes reordered questions so that the conversation flowed. I suppose my approach fell between the 'interview guide' approach and the 'standardized open-ended interview' as described by Cohen (Cohen et al., 2003). In the interview guide approach a list of topics and issues to be covered are drawn up in advance, and the interviewer decides during the interview on the exact wording and order of questions. This means that interviews are conversational and situational: the interviewer has a guide which makes this approach more comprehensive than the 'informal conversational' interview (where questions are spontaneous, and emerge from the conversation) and gaps in the required information can be closed.

With the more informal, less structured approach, there is a danger that important topics may inadvertently be omitted, and the flexibility of the interview could result in interviewees giving very different responses, making comparability of responses difficult. 'Standardized open-ended' interviews enable the interviewer to determine the exact wording and order of questions in advance. All interviewees are asked the same questions in the same order. The two main advantages of this approach over the 'interview guide' approach are that comparability of responses is improved, since all respondents are answering the same question, and that data are complete for each person interviewed. There is, however, a lack of flexibility in relating the interview to particular individuals and circumstances, and the standardized wording of questions can constrain and limit the 'naturalness' and relevance of questions and answers (Cohen et al., 2003, p. 271).

The decision of whether or not to tape-record interviews was made by my interviewees. While audio recording produces a more complete record, I was concerned that those who agreed to be recorded in this way might not feel free to express their views fully. It seems my fears may have been largely unfounded, since the first of my interviewees who allowed our interview to be recorded also offered me on tape his copies of confidential History Working Group documentation. Recording was helpful because due to the flexible nature of the interviews both questions and answers could be 'rambling', making it more difficult to note them verbatim, though that is what I did when interviewees preferred interviews not to be tape-recorded. I used a small recording device (an Olympus micro-cassette Pearlcorder J1), aware that the presence of any mechanical equipment is distracting, and that a smaller device would be less intrusive, and its presence more likely to be forgotten by the interviewee during the interview.

Transcribing

I must admit that when interviewees refused to be recorded, I was privately relieved. I hated hearing my voice on tape! But you do get used to that. Ashley Smith Hammond has written a good deal in her blog about transcribing:

> I've been working away on my transcriptions – and complaining to anyone who will listen . . . after finishing that one on Saturday night it was down to four left . . . it's still down to four left, as I barely managed to get through any yesterday . . . What's holding me up? Well, I've got a bit of a mental block about the one I was working on yesterday. It makes me squirm with embarrassment, transcribing that one. This is the thing about doing your own transcriptions. You have to

listen to your own voice. The voice isn't so much the problem as what I say. I'm judging myself on how I conducted
the interview after the fact. It can engender a lot of self-hate.
I catch myself thinking, 'Shut up! Shut up! Shut up!' every
time I say something on the tape. I can hardly stand to get
through five minutes of interview before I am desperate to
escape and casting about for anything else to do. Like
updating my blog for instance ...

Transcribing speech from a recording machine is time-
consuming and boring. You can get hold of transcribing
machines which, once you get the hang of them, are a useful
tool. But I never used one. So my thumbs used to ache by the
time I got to the end of a transcript – just *play, stop, rewind,* and
play, time after time on my little recorder. You can pay
someone else to do it for you, but if you do it yourself it helps
you to become familiar with the data:

> Another thing I've been noticing is that I can hear things in
> people's voices on the tape that I wasn't tuned in to at the
> time. I can hear the emotion in their voice much more
> clearly when I go back, but I don't really remember being as
> aware of it on the day. When it's going well I enjoy the
> transcription, I remember how the conversation went and
> remember little bits of what I thought or felt. It's like a weird
> déjà vu because I'll get the same feeling or thought listening
> to the tape and then remember that it's the same thing I was
> thinking or feeling on the day.
>
> (Ashley's blog)

Listening to yourself conducting an interview also helps to
improve your interview technique. Ashley wrote:

> I was talking too much and I wished that I would shut up!
> Allowing silences in the conversation doesn't come very
> naturally to me, and I am learning that in this process that is
> something you have to do if you're going to have a good
> interview. People need time to think about what you have
> just asked them.

Cohen et al., stress the importance of transcribing: 'this is a crucial step, for there is potential for massive data loss, distortion and the reduction of complexity' (Cohen et al., 2003, p. 281). They also see the interview as a social encounter and not merely an exercise in data collection. They suggest that one of the main problems with transcripts is that they present the interview as a collection of data rather than as the record of a social encounter. Mishler (1986) has noted that the main disadvantage of audio tapes is that the visual and non-verbal aspects of the interview are not recorded. Morrison (1993, p. 63) recounts an incident where an autocratic headteacher, while talking about the importance of mutual respect and democratic decision making, shook her head vigorously from side to side and pressed the flat of her hand in a downwards motion away from herself, as if to silence discussion! These actions are contextually important, and alter the nature of the data recorded on the audio tape. Video recording would of course provide a more complete account of the interview, since it also records non-verbal communication, but as Cohen et al. note, a videotape is very time-consuming to analyse (Cohen et al., 2003, p. 281). I have not encountered any incident like the one described by Morrison. Even so, I was aware that my transcripts inevitably omitted data from the original encounter.

There are differences between the spoken and written word. When speaking, people might begin the same sentence several times, and will 'um' and 'er' and stop talking in mid-sentence to begin talking about something else. I was not proposing to analyse the speech patterns or undertake any textual analysis. I wanted to compare the responses from interviewees and examine their different accounts in order to build up a picture of what had happened to make the History Working Group change its mind about the inclusion of the Holocaust in the National Curriculum (I discovered early on that the topic was not included in the group's interim report; but it was compulsory in their final report).

Because I was not completing any linguistic or textual analysis I 'tidied up' transcripts, removing some of the hesitations so that they read better. My main aim was to persuade the interviewee to approve the transcript, and let me add their name to their comments. The transcripts are honest representations of the interviews. I included in brackets information that I considered important and relevant. For example, here is a line taken from a transcript of an interview with one of the History Working Group members: 'I think some members of the group were more persuasive than others in the way they talked and had more influence, I'll put it that way (light-hearted laughter)'.

Cohen et al. highlight the importance of recording different kinds of data in the transcript of an audio tape, for example the speaker's tone of voice, the inflection of the voice, short and long pauses and silences, the mood of the speaker, the speed of talk, and so on. Such data are important in complementing the spoken words, and once noted become a matter of interpretation (Cohen et al., 2003, p. 282). Had I not included the bracketed information in the example above, the meaning of what was being said could be interpreted differently. In this example the interviewee demonstrates tact, but implies that particular members of the History Working Group were more influential than others.

Where interviews were not recorded I asked interviewees questions and wrote down their answers verbatim in my notebook. As soon as possible after the interview I typed it up. Once again I cut out 'ums' and 'ers' and indicated in brackets any additional non-verbal information, as well as any notes on the mood and tone of the speaker.

Telephone interviews

Using the telephone to conduct interviews is an effective way of gathering data which is commonly used in survey research. It is a speedy method, and less demanding in terms of time, effort and expense than travelling to meet interviewees. Researchers including Dicker and Gilbert (1988), Nias (1991), Oppenheim (1992) and Borg and Gall (1996) have discussed the merits and disadvantages of telephone interviews. However, interviews conducted over the telephone do pose particular difficulties. It is, for example, very difficult to detect irony over the phone, since you are unable to observe the faces or body language of interviewees. Time on the telephone may also be more limited than in personal meetings. The personal interviews I have conducted were more relaxed, and the conversation more wide-ranging, than those I conducted on the telephone.

One of my phone interviews lasted for 30 minutes, and the other for 40 minutes; while some pleasantries were exchanged, less of a rapport was built with these interviewees than with those I met in person, with whom I spent a good deal more time. Oppenheim talks about the need for the interviewer to be prepared for a telephone interview, and have prompts and probes ready so that the interviewee does not 'dry up' (1992). Although different from face-to-face meetings, the interviews I conducted over the phone were very useful. I prepared in the same way for them as I did for the interviews I conducted in person. Everyone I wanted to talk to was sent a letter. Respondents then contacted me (I gave them my home address as well as the college address, along with my home phone number and email address) to organize an interview.

Making clear what you want

I want to focus on the example I gave in the last chapter about making clear the purpose of the interview. That incident raises several issues – first, obviously, the importance of always making clear the purpose of interviews *and* how you intend to use the data gathered. I wrote up meetings which were 'just for information' as a series of facts, along with any quotes I had been given. These notes were then sent to interviewees to be checked for errors. Such meetings provided a valuable insight into the workings of the groups which revised the National Curriculum for History. Although I couldn't include in my thesis some of the interesting and revealing anecdotes I was told, I gained a greater insight into the selection of these groups and how they worked, which influenced and informed my writing. Had the individuals I met been formally interviewed and named in my thesis, I am convinced the data would have been less rich.

Interviewing elites

Interviewing elites, people currently or formerly in positions of power, is not always easy. Sometimes (especially if they are former elites) they want to talk about their experiences, and do so freely. But others, even those who no longer hold a position of power, are concerned about saying something they shouldn't. Politicians, government ministers and those who serve on government committees have an eye both on the past and the future: how will history perceive their actions, and what can they do now to influence their future image? What about their career – today, and tomorrow? I did not meet any serious difficulties gaining access to members of the History Working Group, though on the whole the members interviewed wished to remain anonymous. Members of the School Curriculum and Assessment Authority Advisory Group for History, and the History Task Group (which reviewed the National Curriculum in 1994 and 1999 respectively) were unwilling to be formally interviewed and identified. But my experience was not unusual: other researchers have found difficulty in gaining access to senior people (Finch, 1986; Hunter, 1993; Ostrander, 1993; Raab, 1987).

Perhaps access to the History Working Group members was easier because they had completed their work some time ago, and in a sense they were former VIPs. Those who continued to hold office posed a greater difficulty in terms of access. Though it was not essential, I would have liked to name all the interviewees I quoted in my thesis. But my priority was gaining access to particular individuals and I was prepared to offer anonymity where requested, mindful of Fitz and Halpin's assertion: 'We still think it is unlikely that civil servants would agree to be involved in policy research unless, or until, anonymity is assured' (1994, p. 36). I raised some sensitive issues with my interviewees, and perhaps for this reason some of them wanted their comments to remain anonymous. I therefore identified some of my interviewees by name, but not others. Where interviewees wished to remain anonymous but gave permission to be quoted, I asked them how they wished to be referred to in the thesis. (For more on interviewing elites see Fitz and Halpin, 1994.)

Can I quote you on that?

A further issue relates to intellectual property. Interviewees cannot demand that material be destroyed. *If* you ask their permission to use data gathered in an interview, they can refuse to give it. I would respect their refusal, but not all colleagues would – and you don't have to.

When I asked one of my interviewees for permission to quote her, she requested not only the draft of the chapter in which I proposed to quote her, but my entire thesis for her to read and approve! This is really not acceptable. Interviewees might decide after the event that they shouldn't have said something, or didn't quite mean something as it was interpreted, and you may decide to give them some 'comeback'. But they really have no right of reply in terms of your thesis and the conclusions you have drawn from what they said. I explained to that particular interviewee that my thesis was not completed, and it would be available for her to read after I had passed my viva.

I didn't hear from her again until, perhaps unwisely, I contacted her to ask about the same quote, which seemed to me inoffensive and uncontroversial – a straightforward description of some work she had done in the field of Holocaust education, my aim being to highlight the pioneering work done by herself and the organization she worked for. This time I wanted permission to use her quote in the book I was writing based on my research.

She telephoned the publisher. She telephoned the college. She ranted and raved. Yet to this day, I do not understand what the problem was. I could have quoted her without her permission, but I had thought it wise to obtain her approval and avoid any problems after publication. I'm glad I did! When the publisher told her of our decision to remove her name and all reference to her from the book (thinking this would please and placate her), she ranted and raved some more! Wouldn't she be given credit for what she had done? The publisher and I stuck with our decision, and eventually the dust settled.

For whatever reason, this interviewee did not like something I had written. There is another lesson here: *not everyone will like what you write*. This is something you have to accept. Your work will be reviewed, critiqued and debated. It's part of the deal. It's not personal. For your own part you should – of course – make sure your research is rigorous. But no one has a right to exert undue influence over what you write. It is *your* work, and you must be true to your writing and to yourself.

Chapter Eight

Have you got 20:20 vision?

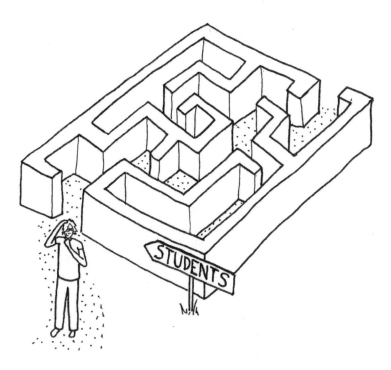

A PhD thesis takes on a life of its own, once you get started. There are many unexpected avenues to explore, sometimes only for you to find that what you thought was an interesting side road is in fact a cul de sac. Professor Clyde Chitty spent about a term researching Shirley Williams's career. In the end, he wrote only relatively few sentences in his thesis containing her name. The only downside to such a digression is the loss of time. The additional subject knowledge may help you feel more confident at the viva (although you should only be questioned on the content of your thesis and the organization of your research). No research is ever wasted. If it doesn't make it into the thesis, it can be saved and turned into an article later. Dr John Lunnun remarked to me that once he had started his PhD, alternative pathways of study opened up, and he was often drawn away 'to read other works that had, at best, tenuous links with my main study but which were fascinating in their own right'. A PhD should allow for one to be self-indulgent and spend time researching topics and personalities who are of interest. That said, it is important to maintain a clear focus on your main subject, or the research may never get finished.

You don't have to work flat-out throughout your PhD. There is time to 'have a life'. (I managed to move home and get married during my studies – in this book, 'my partner' and 'my husband' are the same man.) But the nearer you get to finishing your thesis, the more focused – and selfish – you need to be with your time. Dr Christine Wall notes that 'writing up was a lengthy process, but I was lucky in that I was able to shut myself away in a small study room off the main library at the Institute, where I could escape whenever my real work permitted'. Even if you've been writing throughout, drafting and redrafting chapters of your thesis, you will find that 'pulling it all together' to write the final draft is hard work. Dr Michael Corbett's advice is to 'plan to be incommunicado with your friends and family while you finish [your thesis]' and 'not to take on any big projects, just small regular activities to perhaps lighten the load, like running or going for coffee'. Dr David E. Simpson told me that he doubted 'it is possible to completely hold onto your sanity' at this time:

> I remember one Saturday deciding to take a day off to do something I enjoyed, only to find myself unable to remember what I enjoyed doing! I had a program on my PC which displayed random 'humorous' phrases. One morning my computer greeted me with: 'Maybe your purpose in life is to serve as a warning to others.' It felt like that, too! I realized why handing in the thesis was called 'submission' – I felt like I'd lost a wrestling bout!

Resigning yourself to self-doubt

Self-doubt is a normal part of the PhD process. It comes and goes, and extends from doubting that you can finish your study, to doubting that your study is going to be any good, and finally to doubting – and detesting – other aspects of your life. I wrote in my journal at the beginning of my second term:

> I'm feeling quite lost. I had a lovely Easter holiday but have found it difficult to do anything productive yesterday or today. Perhaps it's just a case of getting back into it. Before Easter I was doing a lot of writing, perhaps I just need to work out what to do next. There is so much to do! I should have gone swimming this afternoon. I feel fat. A swim would have helped me think about what I need to do first. I found out this morning about a conference which starts tomorrow, which looks really good. I'm annoyed I didn't find out about it earlier. I feel very out of it all, and have to try and stop myself from wondering just what the point is ...

At 'down' times like this, remember that although you may *think* everybody else is more worthy than you, cleverer than you, and doing better than you – they're not. Everyone else goes through the same nadirs. If you log on to the student forum at www.findaphd.com, the online PhD community there will be very willing to reassure you that you are far from alone. Online support from other students is helpful because you don't meet face to face and you have a pseudonym, so you can drop the bravado, admit your weaknesses, and be honest about your difficulties. The others are working as hard as you, and feeling just as overwhelmed. No one 'sails through' their PhD, and you don't need to be 'Einstein' to get one. You just need to *want* one. Work hard, and *keep going*. Don't descend into a pit of despair. Even if you don't feel motivated, carry on with your research and writing. And remember the old joke about how to eat an elephant: bit by bit.

Focus on completion

You need to set a date for completion, and work to it. I knew my funding ran out at a certain time, so I was determined to finish by then. But even if you're not worried about funding, it's important to have a date in mind and make every effort to finish the thesis by then, or you can find yourself drifting for years. The longer you live with your PhD, the more likely you'll become dissatisfied with it. I sometimes thought, 'Why did I choose this subject? X, Y or Z would have been a better idea.' But if you're going to get your doctorate, you just have to stay the course, and see the PhD as a beginning rather than an end. I've got a list in my PhD journal of interesting research questions – you can make a note of questions that occur to you while you are doing your doctorate, and research them when you've finished. If you change your focus and go off at different tangents, then before you know it time has lapsed, completion is further away, and you're even more confused.

Professor Victor Newman talks about his experience of writing up the thesis:

> I asked for leave of absence to write my thesis over three months, and developed a writing routine that began very early in the morning, caught up with breakfast and taking my daughter to school, some Tai Chi in the park, and then back to work until after lunch, followed by more writing until 6pm. One of the strange outcomes of the intense introversion that a doctoral thesis involves, combined with dedicated focus on writing, was that I had to junk over 60,000 words that weren't strictly related to my thesis, which proved to be an alternative but related thesis produced in a mental state akin to spirit writing! It was great stuff, but was not developing the hypothesis and it had to go.

When it comes to the final draft, you may well find you need to edit out chunks of writing. I have a computer file named 'bits I've cut from thesis'. It contains 31,000 words! Like Victor, I found I had paragraphs which were good and were related to my subject (I've used a lot of this stuff to write newspaper articles since finishing the PhD). But this writing did not help to develop my thesis, so it had to go.

The role of your supervisor

Good supervision is essential for keeping your thesis on track. Charles believes the problems he encountered during his PhD started with his relationship with his supervisor:

> I attended the 'interview' [for my studentship] and met my supervisor-to-be – not, as I had originally thought, the professor who had taken my [undergraduate] viva, but one of his senior post-docs. Herein lay the seeds of the first problem: his post-doc had not specifically chosen me. Rather, I had effectively been landed on her. 'A very able undergraduate, and willing,' she was assured. I sensed a certain reticence on her part; we didn't click. I'm not sure we ever really did.

My good friend Christine was in the enviable position of being offered, in the same week, two studentships to complete a PhD. 'I don't know how to choose. I didn't expect to get the first one, and I hadn't heard anything from the second place at all. They hadn't even offered me an interview.' She asked a few academics she knew at other universities what they thought, and in the end made her decision based on their advice and the reputation of the supervisor she would be assigned. But when she accepted her place she found her supervisor was on sabbatical and he had a huge number of students, so she would be given joint supervision, and would initially be looked after by her second supervisor.

Christine met with her second supervisor in the first week of her enrolment. She didn't really know what to expect from her supervision, and was happy enough at first. But she grew increasingly uneasy. As dictated by her supervisor, they met fortnightly. She phoned me after one of her supervision sessions, just after Christmas:

> 'Shouldn't I feel more positive and focused after a tutorial – not less? I feel so fed up. I'm trying to be clear and confident

in my tutorials. I start off trying to talk through my ideas, but he cuts me off before I've finished, saying the way I'm planning my research won't work. He recommends endless books and articles I should be reading. A lot of it seems irrelevant. It's like he's pushing me into areas he's more interested in. He sets me all this reading, and asks me to write 'research memos' based on it – which aren't about what I want to do – and then doesn't even talk about the issues I've raised in my writing: he's more interested in correcting my grammar!

'I go into a tutorial wanting to discuss a particular idea, and suddenly he's interrupting – the conversation veers off in another direction. He told me not to do any writing at all last term, just reading! But everyone else I talk to says I should have started writing. I'm worried about falling behind with my study plan. I want to submit my thesis in three years, that's how long my funding lasts. He said it wouldn't matter if I overran. I come out of these meetings feeling I'm not clever enough, and I don't belong here.'

'Is there anyone in the department you can talk to?'

'Maybe, but what can I say?'

'Go to the head of the PhD programme, or someone you trust in the department, and tell them you don't feel it's working out, you're feeling bullied. Be diplomatic, say that he's been great giving up his time for tutorials, but you're feeling suffocated, and do they have any advice ...'

'Perhaps I'm being over-sensitive ... but I'm really fed up with his comments, like "Oh, you should have finished reading that by now. You should be reading a book a week at least." He said he'd help with my quantitative methods paper, but when I showed it to him he said "Oh, this is obviously noddy. You just need to spend a day in the library on it." I honestly don't think he had the first clue how to approach it himself. It's so soul-destroying when I've worked hard on a research memo he set me, and he picks it apart.

Everything I tell him about my research he apparently already knows! He makes me feel stupid.

'I met my principal supervisor the other day, he said to contact this guy at another university, but when I told my second supervisor he said I shouldn't have done that! I talk about prominent people in my field, and he just looks at me blankly – ignores what I've said, and starts talking about something else. I think he wants to shift my work into an area which is more his territory – he *is* very good at what he does. But I've got to do something; I just feel he's the wrong supervisor for me.'

Phillips and Pugh were right when they wrote:

A change of supervisor is the academic equivalent of getting a divorce. There are formal (legal) mechanisms for doing it but the results are achieved, inevitably, only after considerable emotional upset. There are important consequences for the supervisor's professional status and self-esteem if a student initiates a change. Thus it is bound to be a difficult process – often ending with metaphorical blood on the walls.

(E.M. Phillips and Pugh, 1998, pp. 106–7)

But it was lucky that the head of the PhD programme found out how unhappy Christine was, and arranged for her supervisor to be switched early in her second term. There was a new member of the department whose area of expertise was more closely matched with her research interests. The situation needed very careful handling! Even so there were tears and tantrums; phone calls, emails and accusations; a challenge to university regulations on the issue . . . In short, blood *all over* the walls. Christine kept her head down, stayed out of the way, and got on with her work. It was the head of department and the head of the PhD programme who came in for the flak and sorted everything out; but eventually the conflict was resolved, and peace broke out.

It might have been better if Christine had told the supervisor himself how she felt. He suggested as much in an email during the fallout, after she had spoken to the head of the PhD programme. But dealing with a critical supervisor isn't easy.

Christine didn't feel she was able to tell him how she felt – and certainly not face to face, with no one else in the room. How would he have reacted? Her self-esteem was so low that she would probably have blamed herself for how she was feeling. She had nearly broken down in a tutorial, on several occasions. Maybe if her supervisor had seen her in tears he would have changed his approach, at least for a while. But if your self-esteem is already low, it won't be improved by crying in a tutorial.

It had been a hard decision to change supervisor and she felt awful about it, but for Christine it was the right thing to do. If the issue had just been about personality and getting used to her supervisor's way of working, that would have been different. Sometimes, students in these circumstances resolve to 'suffer in silence' and just get on with it. It's not ideal, but if you're confident your supervisor knows what they are doing, but just lacking a good 'bedside manner', then maybe you can decide not to be upset, not to waste your energy wishing the relationship were different, and just get your head down. There should be other staff and students in the department you can bounce ideas off, and get positive responses from.

Dr Mark Tuckett puts the great camaraderie of his research group down to the bullying tactics of his supervisor who, he says, learned from his own supervisor, ('a bullying American workaholic'), 'that the best way of supervising people was to be horrible to them and frighten them into doing the work ... The whole group's general approach was to avoid him as much as possible and rely on each other for help and support. This ... meant that our research group was the most tightly-knit, friendly and cooperative of any of them.'

When Mark began his PhD, he was shocked to find out how hard his supervisor wanted everyone to work: 'He expected everyone to be in the lab from 9 to 6, and most people were in far more than that. I'd say 60 hours a week was pretty standard. There was no way I was going to manage that many hours [at the time, he was recovering from glandular fever] ... I told my supervisor that I was worried. He was initially sympathetic, telling me that if I was efficient and didn't waste time then it was perfectly possible to get enough work done in a normal working week. Although it wasn't much later that he was complaining about my lack of appearance at weekends.'

If you've got a difficult supervisor, like Christine or Mark, you could always *try* talking through your concerns and feelings with them. Perhaps they don't realize how they're making you feel and what you're worried about. You may be pleasantly surprised. And it's preferable to 'blood on the walls'!

Supervision is a two-way process, and Hugh Cunningham describes how his own supervisor instigated a change in supervision:

> I was allocated to Dr Guha. I knew by then fairly precisely what I wanted to do, but he had other ideas. In the middle of our second meeting, he said 'This isn't going to work', and he picked up the phone. He rang John Rosselli, asking him if he would take on this difficult PhD student. I don't think things would be done like this now! John turned out to be an excellent supervisor. He didn't pretend to know very much about my precise topic of research – jingoism in the 1870s – but asked all the right and difficult questions, and let me get on with it.

One reason Hugh had been attracted to Sussex University, where he did his PhD, was that Professor Asa Briggs (now Lord Briggs of Lewes) might have been his supervisor. As it turned out, Briggs had been made Vice Chancellor by the time he got there. If you're going to complete your PhD successfully, your supervisor is key. Dr Alex Cousins thinks it is important to 'choose your supervisor carefully and make sure your personalities are compatible (as far as possible)'. You may not be best friends with your supervisor, but you need to respect and trust them, and they need to understand you.

Mo Mowlam was supervised by Professor Lowenberg who was, in the early 1970s, involved in a research project on legislative politics in Belgium, Switzerland and Italy. This project, writes Julia Langdon, would lead Mo to the subject of her doctorate, 'The impact of direct democracy on the influence of voters, Members of Parliament and interest group leaders in Switzerland'. Langdon describes Mo's relationship with Lowenberg:

He did find that she was a little impatient ... He describes himself as somewhat fussy and orderly in a traditional way. Mo in contrast was energetic, quick and in a fantastic hurry. 'I was fussy about her writing and her prose and I wanted to slow her down a little bit.' He was only partly successful. Claudia Beyer remembers, 'He expected a lot from her and she delivered for him,' but she was also aware of how frustrated Mo could be by her work. She would work very hard and then find she had been marked down because, for example, on one occasion, she had used English rather than American spellings. 'She wondered how she was ever going to survive.' Mo acknowledged the debt she owed Professor Lowenberg in her dissertation, expressing her special gratitude to him – 'who bore with my prose and my impatience in directing this study'. She has said in an interview with the Iowa *Alumni Quarterly* that she lived in awe-tinged fear of him at the time, although she also credits him for valuable lessons in 'tolerance, humanity and decency about human nature'.

(Langdon, 2000, pp. 90–1)

Writing in the *Guardian* in 2002, John Wakeford described the experiences of students who had failed their PhD at the viva. Basically, where students had been unsuccessful, it had been because there was a problem with their supervision. Perhaps they had been assigned the wrong supervisor, or their supervisor hadn't done their job properly. I, like Christine, had a joint supervision, which worked out well for me. I saw both of my supervisors regularly (individually, at least once a term). We sometimes met, all three of us together, perhaps four or five times during the three years I was studying. Both supervisors largely left me to get on with what I was doing, but were on hand and happy to offer advice and guidance. This suited me. But joint supervision isn't easy. There were times when I had conflicting advice from my supervisors, and I had to decide whose advice to choose.

Dr Tania Andrews also had joint supervision, and experienced this problem at a more critical stage:

'I had a phone call from one of my supervisors the day before my viva, saying my conclusion needed rewriting and I shouldn't have submitted my thesis!'

'What did you do?'

'Nothing. My principal supervisor had more experience, and was happy with it. So I just ignored the phone call, and it was fine.'

I wasn't surprised that Christine had found her experience so difficult: the level of supervision she experienced was suffocating. Doing a PhD is unlike taking any other qualification. As Alex Cousins points out, 'You've got to have a massive amount of self-motivation, and be prepared for the fact that it's your responsibility to do the work – no-one will chase you for it.' You can't rely on reading, attending tutorials, writing essays, doing a bit of revision, and turning up for the exam, to get through it. Stuart Foster noted that even though he already had an MA, he 'noticed a huge difference in the quality of what I am expected to show my PhD supervisors when compared to what was acceptable for my Masters dissertation'. PhD research relies on inspiration and serendipity. It's an organic and nebulous process. You need a supervisor to support and guide you. But ultimately, it's down to you.

Rabbi Dr Jonathan Romain had a 'wonderful' relationship with his supervisor 'in that he let me get on with things without any pressure but was always available when I needed to consult. With hindsight, I suppose he could have been more proactive, but then I might have found that irksome.' It's true that some of my friends and colleagues would have found it helpful if their supervisors had 'interfered' a bit more (but not as much as Christine's!); perhaps met them more regularly, and set some deadlines for the completion of chapters.

But there has to be a balance, and an understanding of what works best for each individual student. And if you feel that your supervision isn't working, you mustn't waste time. Christine had a horrible first term, and was really unhappy about her supervision. Changing her supervisor was a traumatic experience – for him, as well as her: he'd put in a lot of work, and was very hurt. But the importance of having the right supervisor can't be stressed enough. John Wakeford warns that 'failure to achieve a PhD had been devastating for these students. Some felt shame, others anger. The majority attributed the failure to inadequacies in supervision – only to discover that this was specifically excluded as grounds for appeal. They should, they were told, have submitted a complaint about that at the time' (Wakeford, 2002).

Seconds out: Submission

After three years, my funding ran out. Before I handed in my thesis, I made sure my supervisors had read it and considered it worthy of submission. I could have carried on refining it, but it was time to stop writing.

The 'problem' of new work being produced all the time, as discussed in Chapter Two, is linked to the issue of finishing and submitting your thesis. The French poet Paul Valery said that 'a poem is never finished; only abandoned'. George Lucas made a similar point about film-making. And pop musician Gary Numan said: 'My albums are always finished by a deadline finally arriving, not because I have made it as good as I think I can make it.' And so it is with writing. You may finish a chapter only to read, or watch, or hear something which adds another dimension to, or contradicts, or supports, something you have written.

Professor Clyde Chitty had just submitted the manuscript for his book about eugenics and education (Chitty, 2007), when he saw Victoria Wood's *Housewife, 49* on television. This drama was based on the Mass Observation diary which Nella Last kept during the Second World War. Mass Observation was started in 1937: these anonymous diaries of volunteers have helped to build up a picture of everyday life in Britain during and after the Second World War. Nella's was one of the first such diaries to be published, in 1981. In her entry for Sunday 19 January 1941 she writes:

> I never thought I'd admire anything that Hitler did, but today, when I read in 'the *Sunday Express*' that he 'painlessly

gassed' some thousands of lunatics, I did so. I believe firmly in euthanasia in incurable cases, whether of cancer, etc., or of mind disease. Far from being cruel, I think it's the reverse – and cruel in the extreme to withhold the 'gift of sleep'. If I ever get to the stage when I would be a burden or endless worry to anyone, I'd 'start off on my own'. Not in any spectacular way – just quietly, with the least possible fuss or bother – and count it no sin. I've often talked to nurses, and heard their views, and been surprised sometimes to find that they coincide with my own – that death should be brought to those who find life too hard to bear. I've heard so often the argument, 'Who is to judge?' or 'Who is to take responsibility?' But then, who is to condemn people to terrible pain – or the horror of incurable insanity and downright madness – and deny the draught that would set them free? I felt like an argument on the subject, and started off, but to my *intense* surprise, my husband agreed heartily, and went further. He said he thought every able-bodied nurse and doctor, and even ordinary people, will have enough to do to succour and bring health to the mentally fit, and that all food and services should be reserved for the sick and wounded.

(Broad and Fleming, 2006, pp. 95–6)

Clyde wanted to point out 'that it was not, in fact, uncommon for some people in Britain to approve of at least *some* of the policies that Hitler was implementing in Germany' (Chitty, 2007, p. 136). He read *Nella Last's War* after watching the television drama, and added a footnote to his manuscript at the last minute after telephoning his publisher: 'It was so relevant I felt I just *had* to include it.'

But at some point, the writing – like the reading – has to stop. There are difficulties associated with going on and on. I suppose the greatest fear of the PhD student is someone else publishing research which is the same as theirs before them; making their own work apparently defunct. It may be that work similar to yours is published while you are completing your research, or just before you submit your thesis or publish your work. But is it really the end of the world? For one thing it shows there is an interest in, and market for, your research. It is highly unlikely that the research will be identical (and if it is, is that necessarily a bad thing? It will support your own findings and lend them greater credence. Or, if you have drawn opposing conclusions, this will add to the debate). More likely, the research will come from a slightly different perspective and may add something to your own work or cast new light on it. You shouldn't expect your own research to be the final word. Remember, you are making a *contribution* to existing knowledge and debate; you are not going to resolve the debate.

Your university will have instructions and notes on how to present your thesis, for example the size of the font and the print layout. The University of London requires all theses to be bound in medium blue cloth and to be lettered in gold on the spine with the degree and year, and your surname and initials in 16- or 18-point type. The binders are familiar with such requirements, but I showed them the written guidelines, just to be sure! Your examinations office should also have a list of binders and their contact details. Queen guitarist Brian May placed a photograph of his thesis, bound in its blue cloth, on his website in August 2007, with the caption 'It doesn't look much, but ...' He handed in his thesis on 3 August 2007:

> Today I finally submit my astronomy thesis to the head of astrophysics at Imperial College. The title is 'Radical Velocities in the Zodiacal Dust Cloud'. I'm not nervous; I don't really get nervous any more. I am just so pleased to hand it in. I started working on this 36 years ago, and over the past few months I have been reassessing it, rewriting it, and covering astronomy from 1974 until now.
>
> (Folkers, 4 August 2007)

Submitting your thesis usually comes as a relief; there is a great feeling of completion. Walking away from Senate House in the October sunshine, having handed in my own thesis, I felt elated but also anxious: what if the examiners did not like my work? (Remember, it doesn't matter whether they agree or disagree with your conclusions as long as your research is rigorous.) What if there was something glaringly obvious that I had missed? (You can only do your best to read everything and cover all the relevant issues.) Were there any typing errors? (I *had* missed a couple: I knew my work so well by the end that when I proofread it I saw what *should* be on the page, rather than what was actually there.) One precaution answers many of these concerns: get somebody else to read through your thesis for you, well before you have to submit it.

I had submitted my thesis. It was too late to worry about anything. Now, it was a waiting game.

Chapter Nine

Don't leave hostages to fortune

A PhD viva is a bit like a criminal trial.

> 'You are charged with putting yourself forward as a successful PhD candidate: capable of designing, completing and analysing research which makes an original contribution to existing knowledge and debate on your chosen topic. How do you plead?'

> 'Guilty.'

Using the evidence (your thesis), you present your defence to the two examiners, who are – by turns – counsel for the prosecution, judge, and jury. You are the counsel for your own defence. There is one internal examiner (often a member of staff from your own department but who has not had any involvement with you or your work) and one external examiner (who holds greater sway than the internal examiner and is an expert in your field from another university). It is a good idea to discuss with your supervisor who you think you would like to invite to be your examiners: just as in a real trial, where defendants and their legal teams have the right to challenge and reject a member of the jury in order to ensure they get a fair trial, so you too have an input into who is on your 'jury'.

Who do you think would be a suitable person to examine your thesis? The choice of external examiner – because they hold most sway – needs to be considered carefully. It doesn't need to be someone with whom you have totally agreed in your thesis, or someone whose writing you have heavily criticized; but it is helpful if they know your field and are sympathetic to your methodology. This is not a decision you should be asked to make alone. If you trust your supervisor, be guided by their opinion. A good supervisor, like a good barrister, is experienced in the process and 'knows the ropes'. This is their job – do you think you know better than them? One student I know had friends who were qualified to be her viva examiners, and she asked them to do so despite the misgivings of her supervisor. It was a disastrous decision! For whatever reason – possibly because the examiners did not want to be accused of nepotism – the viva was difficult, and in the end the candidate was given 18 months to make major revisions to her work before resubmitting it and having to go through a second viva.

Examiners (unlike barristers) are not paid well for their services. They get about £40 for reading your thesis and examining it. They don't do it for the money. They do it because it is expected of them and they anticipate the favour being returned for their own students. This makes it all rather a delicate business involving egos, friendships and careers. Examiners are aware that if they give you a particularly hard time, and later ask your supervisor to examine one of their students, their student may get an equally hard time in return. A good viva is more like a seminar than an interrogation. Sometimes candidates are told the result before the viva, which makes the experience more relaxed, and this practice is becoming increasingly common. The viva usually takes at least a couple of hours, and three or four is not unusual. This might sound like a long time, but because you're so involved in this rather intense exchange it's like a party you've been looking forward to, and you don't want to end – but it seems to flash past in the blink of an eye. It isn't like spending four hours in a doctor's waiting room. Well, not like your local GP's surgery. But of course, in a way you *are* in a doctor's waiting room ...

At some universities you can take your supervisor with you as a 'court room observer'. Although they can't make any comment, their presence can be reassuring, and it may be useful to have someone to take notes. As in a real trial, it is the responsibility of the counsel for the defence to convince the jury of their case. So your performance in the viva may be as important as your thesis! The examiners will have judged the thesis before they meet you – but a strong performance at the viva could sway them if they were unconvinced about parts of your thesis. Equally, a weak performance might make them question their inclination towards passing you. The viva is about the examiners checking that the thesis is your own work and making sure you understand what you did.

Usually, the examiners are as much on your side as they can be. Victor Newman said of his experience as an external examiner:

> I have to admit to having bent the category of 'conditional pass', involving in effect the writing and rewriting of key chapters within a thesis, when I realized that the supervisor had been negligent, and the candidate had lost their job, lost a child and was in the process of being divorced. This meant the advice to the candidate had to be very specific, with several pages of notes. I honestly think the alternative might have involved suicide, and I felt the university had let the candidate down.

Victor also recalled a 'campus rumour' that as an internal examiner at Cranfield University he had thrown a doctoral thesis out of the viva examination window. He explained that in fact, 'when after three days of trying to find the nuggets of gold in a thesis and being face to face with the candidate, I asked "When you presented your thesis were you aware that it did not meet the criteria for a doctoral thesis?" the candidate nodded in glum agreement ... I concluded the viva at that point.' So, no thesis actually flying through the air, but the metaphorical equivalent of the candidate's work being sent flying. Before you submit your thesis you need to prepare for your viva.

So that they are sure of their verdict, your examiners will cross-examine you on the evidence you have submitted. This means your thesis must be watertight. Anything you have failed to include – for whatever reason – is inadmissible. Anything you have included, you must be prepared to be questioned on. Don't leave anything hanging. Go through your thesis and identify any potential minefields so that you 'don't leave hostages to fortune'. This was a favourite phrase of one of my supervisors.

Constructing your argument

The same supervisor was also fond of telling me that my thesis could actually have been two separate PhD studies. He was right. I could have completed my whole PhD on the history of the Holocaust as a topic on the National Curriculum for History. But my starting point had been what was taught in the classroom. I wanted to track the policy into practice.

What I discovered was that the confusion at the policy level, over what the aims and objectives of teaching the Holocaust in school history were, was reflected among history teachers in the classroom. And that is how my other supervisor and I decided to link the two parts of my study. My concluding sentences read:

> It is difficult to establish a direct link between a lack of clarity regarding the rationale behind the inclusion of the Holocaust among those who have shaped the National Curriculum for History, and the variety of motives that surround the teaching of the topic in Key Stage 3 [pupils aged 11 to 14] history. Yet it is clear that the debate surrounding how the Holocaust should be understood and presented in history lessons is complex, and it seems the lack of a rationale contributes to the wide variety of ways in which the topic of the Holocaust is approached by history teachers.
>
> (L. Russell, 2005, pp. 231–2)

Had I not drawn this conclusion, and thus connected the two parts of my study, I might have been questioned at my viva on why I had chosen to look at both of these areas, and whether and how I thought the two might be connected. To make my thesis 'watertight', I included statements like this:

> My thesis, particularly the following chapter, draws upon and provides an overview of some of the literature on the topic of the Holocaust. Given the size of the bibliography of works on this period of history, and the fact that this thesis is not principally about the Holocaust but rather how the topic is approached in school history, I have not endeavoured to read this entire bibliography. I have read some of this literature as well as literature on the topic of teaching the Holocaust in

history. Based on this reading I have developed the issues that seem to me interesting and germane. This has been particularly necessary in order to maintain a clear focus, but readers may identify issues that have not been pursued but they feel warrant attention.

(L. Russell, 2005, p. 54)

So actually, you don't so much *write* a PhD thesis as *construct* it.

How do you prepare for a viva?

My viva took place five months after I had submitted my thesis. There were unfortunately a couple of delays for health reasons. My lead supervisor had to have heart surgery, so my viva was first scheduled for February. But then the external examiner had to cancel it because she got shingles. The viva was rescheduled for March. When the day came I found I was almost as nervous as on my wedding day. (But not as nervous as I was for my driving test. 'I can come with you and sit in the back of the car,' said my instructor. I was shaking with fear and couldn't stop crying. No, thanks. That would have been an extra pressure. When I passed, the only person more surprised than me was my instructor. But during my viva, having my supervisors there in the room boosted my confidence.)

In fact, my viva was far from being a horror story. It was what a viva should be, an opportunity to discuss and debate the issues my work had raised – like a seminar. Dr David E. Simpson said he really enjoyed his four-hour viva 'because it was the first time in four years that there were people [to talk to] who weren't allowed to walk off while I was talking about my work!' His thesis title was 'Maximum entropy image processing in two and three dimensional single photon nuclear medicine imaging'. If you want to talk about your work without people's eyes glazing over – as well as to help you preserve your sanity, and prepare for your viva (where it could be a question) – then work out a single-sentence response to: 'What is your thesis about?' That way you won't be standing on your own at parties for the three or four years of your doctoral research.

Dr Charles Campbell's viva was also delayed slightly, but not on health grounds:

I received an email requesting my attendance at 8 a.m. one Thursday morning. I believe it is customary for vivas to be held in a student's own department – a familiar setting, to ease nerves. But my internal examiner was unable to make it across London and so I was asked if I would mind going to him. It meant a 6 a.m. start to get there. Not ideal, but I didn't mind. I was confident. I knew my specific subject inside out, and almost certainly better than anybody else. One might even say I was spoiling for a fight. But there is always the broader subject which threatens to trip up the overly-confident candidate, and I still feared I might end up like one of the students of PhD folklore: the ones who fail their viva and consequently their PhD outright. No retakes; no excuses. Three years of hard work for nothing! Only a fool would enter their viva without any concerns whatsoever.

I waited in a deserted corridor, nervously fiddling with my tie, clutching a copy of my thesis. 8 a.m. came and went. At 8.45 a man finally appeared. He was wearing a fluorescent cycling jacket over his suit, and threw me a quizzical glance as he passed me.

'Can I help you?' he asked. I explained who I was. He looked aghast.

'But you're not expected until Monday!' he replied.

My face flushed at the prospect of having made such a stupid error. I rechecked the printout of the email I had been sent. It said Thursday, and gave that day's date. It transpired that his secretary had made a mistake. He apologized profusely, and I assured him that it was no problem (what else could I do?!). I phoned my girlfriend: 'That was quick!' she exclaimed. It was still only a little after 9 a.m. I told her they'd given me the wrong day. She didn't believe me. The pinnacle moment of my student career would just have to wait.

A nervous weekend came and went, and I eventually found myself back in that same corridor on Monday at 8 a.m. Take two! I doubt that the professors were lenient on me as a result of the date debacle, although most students are probably not welcomed with an apology as they take their seats. They congratulated me on a well-constructed thesis and then began a rapid, quick-fire cross-examination. Two hours later I was out. The nightmare prospect of a nine-hour interrogation was not to be. I was a fully-fledged member of the scientific community, PhD tagged after my name, two research papers in press, and a grant to fund further research.

Victor Newman says of his own viva:

> I can't remember much about it, apart from the terror and my rapid conclusion from the questioning that the external examiner hadn't read it. I was surprised by the apparent silliness of the questions at the time, which on reflection I realize were about inviting me to restate the hypothesis, the proofs and the methodologies involved. This goes to show how autistic and introvert the lone researcher can become. As a result, I always rehearsed the viva [with my own students] and facilitated the candidate in critiquing their own work, its strengths and weaknesses, to reduce the stress-level and help them to be more articulate and enjoy the viva itself.

It is a good idea for research students to present and discuss their ideas in groups. A mock viva with other students or academics from your department can also be helpful. This will help you to practise defending your thesis, and their critiques could be useful. Talking about my work clarified my thinking and gave me greater confidence, because once I started talking about what I was doing and why, ideas flowed – I began to realize I knew more than I thought I did.

When I was given a date for my viva, I thought about doing some preparation. But how? Not everyone does prepare; for instance, Professor David Bellamy said that he had 'no need' to because he 'had done the research'. Viva preparation is psychological rather than practical. You will find advice on preparing for your viva in books like *How to Get a PhD*, where Phillips and Pugh suggest revising your thesis:

> First you take a maximum of three sheets of feint-ruled A4 paper (try to manage with two if you can). You draw a straight vertical line down the centre of each sheet. You now have two sets of about 35 lines, i.e. 70 half-lines. Each half-line represents one page of your thesis. Now you number each half-line. One to 35 are the left-hand lines and 36–70 are the right-hand half-lines on the first sheet of paper.

> Next, you take your time, say about two weeks, to write on every half-line the main idea contained on the corresponding page of your thesis.
>
> (E.M. Phillips and Pugh, 1998, p. 140)

I am hopeless at following instructions of any kind, probably because I haven't got the patience to read them properly. I don't doubt that this method works well for many, and would enable you to make a thorough revision of your thesis. But it reminded me of the Victoria Wood programme, *Val de Ree*, where she and Jackie (Celia Imrie) are trying to put up a tent:

> Jackie: Right. Start again. Take Tube A and apply to Bracket D with the flange channel outermost.

> Victoria: Outermost. I've done that.

> Jackie: (*mumbling*) Figure three . . . repeat with tubes B, F and J.

> Victoria: Yes.

> Jackie: Figure four – then *quasi* tighten Socket Cap E until semi-protruding Locking Hinge K is engaged.
>
> (Wood, 1990, p. 121)

Rabbi Dr Jonathan Romain said he found it difficult to prepare for his viva 'in that I have a very poor memory (not a great asset for a research student, especially a historian!) and once I write anything it goes out of my mind, as if my brain says "job done – now delete information no longer required" – so I had to re-read my thesis several times before the viva so as to remind

myself what it was all about.' I have the same problem: I seem
to be able to retain factual information for as long as I am using
it, and then my brain seems to file it away. I was worried that in
the five months between submitting my thesis and doing my
viva I would forget everything I had done. So, I decided to
prepare for my viva by making a list of questions which I
expected to come up, and writing a response to each one. To
help me do this, I also found out as much as I could about my
examiners, and read as much of their work, as possible – even if
it wasn't completely relevant. I thought this would help me to
work out where they were 'coming from'. I reasoned that they
were likely to focus on the parts of my thesis which matched
their own areas of interest and idiosyncrasies. I had cited in my
thesis one or two books written by my lead examiner; it doesn't
really matter whether you have done this or not – but it may
help to flatter egos.

In hindsight, I don't think I would actually have forgotten
everything. But thinking about possible questions and answers
for the viva gave me something to do and meant I was reading
and revising my thesis a bit, if not as thoroughly as suggested by
Phillips and Pugh. Here are some of the notes I made:

What is your thesis? What is original about your research?
- My work makes a contribution to the debate on teaching
  the Holocaust – I have emphasized what I consider to be
  most important. The work on how the Holocaust came to
  be included in the Final Report is, to the very best of my
  knowledge, completely original: this account is not
  otherwise available in the public domain. It is not detailed
  in the History Working Group minutes. This thesis also
  reveals the muddle of classroom practice over this topic.
- History teachers lack clarity. Is their rationale social, moral
  or historical? This lack of clarity is also reflected at the
  policy-making level.

Isn't this two PhDs?
- As I state in the opening paragraph in Chapter Two, the
  reasons for the prominent position of this topic in the
  National Curriculum for History, and what history teachers see as being important about the topic of the

Holocaust, appear to be related. The lack of clarity at the policy level is reflected in the lack of clarity in the history classroom.

- I wanted to see how the position of the topic of the Holocaust on the National Curriculum for History had been interpreted by teachers, and whether my experience was reflected in the history classroom more widely. As a history teacher I felt the practical implications were important.

What prompted you to complete this research?

- As stated on page 17, anecdotal evidence seemed to support Kinloch's assertions [the Holocaust is approached differently from other topics in history; there is confusion over objectives; and the topic is often taught primarily for social and moral rather than for historical reasons]. As I write on pages 21 and 22, I also struggled to teach this topic. Is it anti-racist education? Is it genocide prevention? ... Should the Holocaust be taught in school history for social, moral or historical purposes?
- It does not surprise me that Susan Hector's research has revealed that religious education teachers and history teachers are teaching the same lessons with the same objectives. I taught both subjects and on one occasion used the same lesson plan for a history and an RE lesson (p. 195, Chapter Six).

I made several pages of notes like this. A lot of the questions I identified did not come up in the viva. There were some that surprised me and I had to think quickly, but this was OK because I was warmed up by the time they were thrown at me – in fact, the very first question I was asked was the very first question in my notes. It was a question I had anticipated, and I was ready with a rehearsed answer. After that one was out of the way satisfactorily, I relaxed a bit. You could, if you wanted, take notes like these into the viva with you. But all I took was a copy of my thesis, in which I had made some brief notes (taken from my list of possible questions and answers) on Post-it stickers.

Like Charles Campbell's, my own PhD was awarded straight

after my viva. This is the first of a series of possible outcomes. The second – which is more common – is that you are told straightaway that you have passed, but that you will have to make some corrections or amendments: maybe a point has not been referenced to the satisfaction of the examiners. For instance – and I know someone who found themselves in this position – you may have been given access to confidential official papers, and asked not to specify how you sourced the material. In such a case you would have to find a way of referencing the papers to the satisfaction of your examiners, while protecting your source. This could have been an issue for me, but I was offered access to the same material (the minutes of the History Working Group meetings) by two sources – one which I was asked not to divulge, and another where anonymity was required, but where a precedent had been set by a previous researcher working in the field. So when I needed to explain how I accessed the minutes, I was able to note that I had done so by the same means as Robert Phillips during his earlier research (R. Phillips, 1998b).

Any amendments you need to make to your thesis are overseen by your internal examiner. You usually have about a month to resubmit the thesis, and you may have to do another viva. Although this is disappointing, it is not disastrous because once you have your doctorate, it's yours! Nobody need know about the hoops you had to jump through to get it.

There is a further possibility: your examiners may judge that you've done enough to earn an MPhil, and so award you with that instead. But this shouldn't happen if your supervisor knows what they are doing, and what is required for you to earn your PhD. But don't forget that you *can* fail a PhD, and this would be a disaster after all your hard work. It shouldn't happen, but sometimes it does. With good supervision, it shouldn't happen to you.

After successfully completing his viva, Dr Brian May said: 'I'm feeling rather joyful. I can't tell you how much of a weight off the mind it is.' He said of his viva experience: 'It was a bit nerve-racking walking into the room, but once we got going it was fascinating ... There's always that feeling they could ask that big question that could sink you, but luckily they didn't.' (Associated Press, 24 August 2007). He wrote on his website:

> Yes. It's done, and after about 37 years, I am finally a doctor. The oral examination of my thesis, and of me, lasted about three hours, and then I retired with Professor Rowan-Robinson, for a few moments, for my two examiners to confer. After only a couple of minutes they called me back into the room and offered their hands in congratulations. Yes, my category was number two. I understand pretty much nobody gets a first category – which is 'This is perfect, here's your PhD.'

> Mine is: 'We like it. Make these adjustments, and it's yours.'

> The categories after this say things like: 'Go write it up again', or 'Go and do some more research', or 'Why not have an MPhil instead?'! ... all the way down to number eight – which is basically: 'Forget it !!!' (This is all paraphrased of course!)

> So I am very happy. I celebrated at the Hard Rock Cafe with my family and my professors.
>
> (May, 24 August 2004)

What is important about PhD research?

I remember, like Brian May, being very happy and relieved after my viva. It really is a weight off the mind. Victor Newman talked about 'bending the rules' for a particular student whose circumstances were unusually distressing. For most PhD students, the experience is testing enough without additional personal problems. Professor Hugh Cunningham suggests what is most important about PhD research is recovering from it! 'Too many students get so bogged down in the research itself, or in the possibly relevant theory, that they lose sight of the larger picture.' Recovery can take some time, as Dr Sarah Watkins explains:

> I recently completed a DPhil at Oxford in Modern Languages. I found the whole experience really bewildering and

confidence-crushing, to the point that I decided to opt out of academia altogether. I'm now teaching in a secondary school in Oxford city, and am only just beginning to get my head round starting to write again (hopefully for educational publications). My thesis is going to be published soon, and it's very strange how I experienced the whole process as so awful, and yet what came out of it is seemingly very good.

Sarah is not the only PhD to turn their back on academia. Despite his success and the grant to fund further research, Charles Campbell found that:

The lack of support, of praise, reward or encouragement had taken their toll. Others better than me might be able to handle it, but I suspected I would not. Six months later I accepted a new position outside of academia (though still scientifically related) and departed the lab down that one-way street. I certainly had a greater self-awareness, and a more controlled – perhaps realistic – confidence. I had added a drop to the ocean of scientific endeavour, and felt ready to go in search of other challenges, armed with a belief that no matter how hopeless any project can seem at any given time, things can and will work out. Eventually. And it was this that allowed me to give everything up two and half years later and set off on a 14-month honeymoon – my wife's reward for sticking by me through those dark, miserable days of self-doubt, disillusionment and hopelessness of my mid-PhD crisis.

A PhD is a life-changing personal journey. It is the mental equivalent of running the London marathon, or swimming the Channel. My PhD led me to question almost everything I had once taken for granted. The process is a challenge, and it is sometimes torturous, but ultimately wonderful because you emerge liberated. Afterwards, anything is possible. You learn how to think. You can see daily routines for what they are – structures to help us organize ourselves, but not to be followed slavishly. After finishing his PhD, Charles thought nothing of dropping everything and taking a 14-month honeymoon. There is a postscript overleaf about life after your PhD. Victor

Newman is right when he says: 'Doing a doctorate is a bit like Special Forces selection. The process itself can change you. It is very much about the journey, and not about arriving. And, if you are lucky, the journey will continue for the rest of your life.'

The hard work is worth it.

Stock up on the jelly babies, and go for it. And good luck!

Life after your PhD. A postscript

I have just taken a break from my writing for a late lunch. *Murder She Wrote* has just finished on the TV. There is something about the lifestyle of its heroine Jessica Fletcher, a retired teacher turned author, which appeals to me. She's a bestselling novelist living by the sea. I live by the sea. I haven't written any bestselling novels, or helped the police to solve any murders. It is also unlikely that either of my books is going to be a runaway bestseller to rival the success of Jessica Fletcher's crime fiction. Nonetheless, I do feel I have a certain affinity with Jessica, and have always been drawn to her Cabot Cove lifestyle (minus the murders).

'So, what are you going to do when you finish?' As a PhD student, that's a question you'll be asked regularly and often. I had hoped to turn my thesis into a book after my PhD, and once my viva was over, that's what I started planning. You may not feel like it during your research, but you will have a post-PhD life. As is noted above, what Hugh Cunningham thinks is important about PhD research is recovering from it: 'Too many students get so bogged down in the research itself, or in the possibly relevant theory, that they lose sight of the larger picture.'

Gaining a PhD is the beginning. Although in those last few months your thesis is all-consuming, it is a good idea to consider your post-PhD life along the way. It helps your rehabilitation (it sounds dramatic, but it's apt!) to have some ideas about what you want to do next. The post-viva euphoria can quickly give way to a sense of anti-climax. You may want to take a break, but it will help if you have a project to focus on. You'll find that you suddenly have a lot of time to fill.

Unlike academic journal articles, you will get paid for writing a book. But writing academic books doesn't pay much. In fact, unless you're a best-selling author book-writing in general doesn't pay well. You write a book for the love of it, or because you hope to be the next J.K. Rowling, as Clive James said in his *A Point of View* on BBC Radio 4, after the publication of the seventh *Harry Potter*:

> … Most writers don't even make a living. Although the occasional book of mine does reasonably well, about, say

0.003 on the Rowling scale, I'm always careful not to tell a journalist how many copies it has sold, because the journalist invariably looks unimpressed.

Journalists are too used to hearing that Jeffrey Archer or John Grisham sold a million of their latest book in a week. But the average book doesn't sell even a thousand copies in a year.

. . . If would-be writers aren't capable of writing a book for its own sake, they shouldn't be writing at all. I speak as one who would have found it hard to make ends meet as a writer if I had not been wearing another hat in show business. I can't honestly whinge about having pushed my pen in vain, but if I had done nothing else except write books I would be raking the leaves on one of J.K.'s front lawns by now, and glad of the gig.

And I'm one of the lucky ones.

(C. James, 2007, 29th July)

On average, for paperbacks authors receive 10 per cent of the net receipts (how much the publishers sell the book for – not the cover price), rising to 12 per cent after a certain number of copies have sold. This percentage is lower for hardback copies. Having successfully pitched an idea to a publishing house, you will be sent a contract. Royalties are negotiated on a contract-by-contract basis. How close you get to the average depends on how much the publishers want your book; how well known you are; what the commercial market is; and whether there is any competition for your manuscript. I have a colleague who said he wanted 10 per cent for his last book, or he wouldn't write it. He got his percentage. But the 'throwing your toys out of the pram' strategy might be better left until later in your writing career. You may consider it better to take a lower percentage, get your book published and your name known, and try for a better deal next time.

Most publishing houses have guidelines on their website for the submission of book proposals. There is a chicken-and-egg scenario about whether you get your contract first and then write the book, or write a book first and then find a publishing contract. I have one friend currently writing a book and planning to find a publisher when it is finished, and another friend who would not consider writing any more than a proposal before signing a contract.

If you're not sure which publishing house to go for, have a look at the sort of books on their lists. What have they published recently? This might give you an idea of whether your book would appeal to them. Your PhD supervisor, or someone else in your department, may also have some suggestions, or even contacts at particular publishing houses.

If you're reading this before you embark on a PhD, thinking about writing a book proposal may seem a faraway notion. But once you've got your PhD, you'll be a different person – with a new-found confidence. Writing a book – if that is what you want to do – will not seem an insurmountable task. After what you have achieved, nothing will seem insurmountable.

I used not to like speaking in public, because it made me very nervous. If I could avoid speaking up in seminars as an undergraduate, or at staff meetings as a teacher, then I would. When I began my PhD, I would feel a knot in my stomach just thinking about telephoning interviewees to organize a meeting. I sometimes still feel slight apprehension before I speak in public; but having finished the PhD, I'm happy to do it. Not long after I finished, the deputy head at my former secondary school telephoned to ask if I would be the guest speaker at the school Certificate Evening. I didn't hesitate to say yes! And when I was asked to interview former Education Minister Stephen Twigg for a piece in the *Times Educational Supplement*, I had no qualms about making the necessary calls.

Unexpected opportunities, which you can explore with new-found confidence, are likely to come your way too as a result of your study.

Seize them, and enjoy your journey.

References

Alexander, T. (producer) (2007), *The Verdict*. BBC 2.

Amos, J. (2005, 9 September), 'Winston warns of stem cell "hype"'. BBC News.

Assinder, N. (2007, 9 July), 'How significant is Campbell diary?' http://news.bbc.co.uk/1/hi/uk_politics/6284062.stm: BBC News.

Associated Press (2007, 24 August), 'Rocker gets doctorate 30 years late'. *The New York Times*, online edition, *www.nytimes.com*.

Baty, P. (2003, 9 May), 'Clarke lays into useless history'. The *Times Higher Education Supplement*.

BBC News (2007, 3 August), 'Queen star hands in science PhD'. http://news.bbc.co.uk/1/hi/entertainment/6929290.stm.

Bell, J. (1999), *Doing Your Research Project: A Guide for First-time Researchers in Education and Social Science* (third edn). Buckingham: Open University Press.

Borg, W.R. and Gall, M.D. (1996), *Educational Research: An Introduction* (sixth edn). New York: Longman.

Brand, J. (2004), *Sorting Out Billy*. London: Headline.

—— (2005), *It's Different for Girls*. London: Headline.

Bresheeth, H., Hood, S. and Jansz, L. (2000), *Introducing the Holocaust*. Cambridge: Icon Books.

Broad, R. and Fleming, S. (eds) (2006), *Nella Last's War*. London: Profile Books.

Butler, J. (1990), *Gender Trouble: Feminism and the Subversion of Identity*. London: Routledge Classics.

Cannadine, D. (ed.) (2002), *What is History Now?* Hampshire: Palgrave Macmillan.

Carr, E.H. (1961), *What is History?* London: Macmillan.

Castellini, C., Mugnai, C. and Dal Bosco, A. (2002), 'Effect of organic production on broiler carcass and meat quality'. *Meat Science 60*, 219–25).

Chitty, C. (2007), *Eugenics, Race and Intelligence in Education*. London: Continuum.

Cohen, L., Manion, L. and Morrison, K. (2003), *Research Methods in Education* (fifth edn). London and New York: Routledge Falmer.

Colley, L. (2002), *Captives: Britain, Empire and the World 1600–1850*. London: Jonathan Cape.

—— (2002, 17 October), *In Our Time*: BBC Radio 4.

Crane, R. (2007), *The Last Confession*. London: Oberon Books.

Creme, P. and Lea, M.R. (1997), *Writing at University: A Guide for Students*. Buckingham: OUP.

Dewhurst, R.J., Fisher, W.J., Tweed, J.K.S. and Wilkins, R.J. (2003), 'Comparison of grass and legume silages for milk production. 1. Production responses with different levels of concentrate'. *Journal of Dairy Science 86*, 2598–611.

Dicker, R. and Gilbert, J. (1988), 'The role of the telephone in educational research'. *British Educational Research Journal 14*(1), 65–72.

Earnshaw, S. (2006), *Existentialism: A Guide for the Perplexed*. London: Continuum.

Ellis, K.A., Innocent, G., Grove-White, D., Cripps, P., McLean, W.G., Howard, C.V. *et al.* (2006), 'Comparing the fatty acid composition of organic and conventional milk'. *Journal of Dairy Science 89*, 1938–50.

Elton, G.R. (1991), *Return to Essentials. Some Reflections on the Present State of Historical Study*. Cambridge: Cambridge University Press.

Evans, R.J. (1997), *In Defence of History*. London: Granta Books.

Evans, R.J. (2002), 'What is History? – Now', in D. Cannadine (ed.), *What is History Now?* (pp. 1–18). Hampshire: Palgrave Macmillan.

Evans, R.J. (2003), *The Coming of the Third Reich*. London: Allen Lane.

Finch, J. (1986), *Research and Policy: The Use of Qualitative Methods in Social and Educational Research*. London: Falmer Press.

Fitz, J. and Halpin, D. (1994), 'Ministers and mandarins: Educational research in elite settings', in G. Walford (ed.), *Researching the Powerful in Education* (pp. 32–50). London: UCL Press.

Folkers, M. (2007, 4 August), 'My week: Queen guitarist Brian May'. *Independent*.

Gash, N. (1961), *Mr. Secretary Peel: The Life of Sir Robert Peel to 1830*. London: Longman.

—— (1972), *Sir Robert Peel: The Life of Sir Robert Peel after 1830*. London: Longman.

—— (1979), *Aristocracy and People: Britain 1815–1865*. London: Edward Arnold.

Gibson, O. (2007, 12 February), 'TV dietician to stop using title Dr in adverts'. *Guardian*.

Giedroyc, M. (2006), *Going Ga Ga: Is There Life After Birth?* London: Ebury Press.

Haydn, T. (2000), 'Teaching the Holocaust through history', in I. Davies (ed.), *Teaching the Holocaust: Educational Dimensions, Principles and Practice* (pp. 135–49). London: Continuum.

Hensher, P. (2007, 13 February), 'You can trust me, I'm a doctor . . . It's always been a great puzzle why the Home Secretary likes to be referred to as "Dr John Reid" '. http://comment.independent.co.uk/columnists_a_l/philip_hensher/article2264664.ece: *Independent*.

Hitchcock, G. and Hughes, D. (1995), *Research and the Teacher: A*

Qualitative Introduction to School-based Research (second edn). London: Routledge Falmer.

Hunter, A. (1993), 'Local knowledge and local power: Notes on the ethnography of local community elites'. *Journal of Contemporary Ethnography 22*, 36–58.

Ireland On-line (15 July 2007), 'May completes his PhD thesis'. http://breakingnews.iol.ie/entertainment/story.asp?j=225281776&p=zz 5z8z48z.

Jahan, K., Paterson, A. and Spickett, C.M. (2006), 'Relationships between flavour, lipid composition and antioxidants in organic, free-range and conventional chicken breasts from modelling'. *International Journal of Food Sciences and Nutrition 57*, 229–43.

James, C. (2007, 29 July), 'J.K. Rowling, the new Roger Bannister', *A Point of View*. http://news.bbc.co.uk/1/hi/magazine/views/a_point_of_view/ (BBC).

James, J. (12 May 2004), 'Brand at her best in Bristol'. http://www.bbc.co.uk/bristol/content/readingroom/2004/05/12brand.shtml: BBC.

Jenkins, K. (1991), *Rethinking History*. London: Routledge.

Johnson, P. (2002), 'If ontology, then knowledge: Catching up with webont'. http://www.xml.com/cs/user/view/cs_msg/635.

Kettle, M. (1990, 4 January), *Guardian*.

Keyes, M. (2001), *Under the Duvet*. London: Michael Joseph.

Langdon, J. (2000), *Mo Mowlam, The Biography*. London: Little, Brown and Company.

Levi, T. (2003), *Did you ever meet Hitler, Miss?* London: Vallentine Mitchell.

Lofland, J. (1971), *Analyzing Social Settings*. New York: Wadsworth.

MacIntyre, D. (1999), *MacIntyre: One Man . . . Four Lives . . . Undercover*. London: BBC Worldwide.

Marlow, J. (1969), *The Peterloo Massacre*. London: Rapp and Whiting.

Marr, A. (2004), *My Trade: A Short History of British Journalism*. London: Macmillan.

Marwick, A. (2001), *The New Nature of History: Knowledge, Evidence, Language*. Basingstoke: Palgrave.

May, B. (2004, 24 August), 'It's done'. http://www.brianmay.com/brian/brianssb/brianssb.html.

McCall Smith, A. (2007, 7 August), Newsletter. http://www.alexander mccallsmith.co.uk/archive.html.

—— (2007), *The World According to Bertie: A 44 Scotland Street Novel*. Edinburgh: Polygon.

Mishler, E.G. (1986), *Research Interviewing: Context and Narrative*. Cambridge MA: Harvard University Press.

Morrison, K.R.B. (1993), *Planning and Accomplishing School-centred Evaluation*. Norfolk: Peter Francis.

Morton, A. (1998), *Diana: Her True Story – In Her Own Words*. London: Michael O'Mara Books.

Nias, J. (1991), 'Primary teachers talking: A reflexive account of longitudinal research', in G. Walford (ed.), *Doing Educational Research* (pp. 147–65). London: Routledge.

Oppenheim, A.N. (1992), *Questionnaire Design, Interviewing and Attitude Measurement*. London: Pinter Publishers.

Ostrander, S. (1993), ' "Surely you're not in this just to be helpful?" Access, rapport, and interviews in three studies of elites'. *Journal of Contemporary Ethnography 22*, 7–27.

'Our Faith on Sunday' (2006). Cheshire: The Catholic Printing Company of Farnworth.

Paechter, C. (2003), 'On goodness and utility in educational research', in P. Sikes, J. Nixon and W. Carr (eds), *The Moral Foundations of Educational Research: Knowledge, Enquiry and Values*. Buckingham: Open University Press.

Paris, E. (2002), *Long Shadows: Truth, Lies and History*. London: Bloomsbury.

Parsons, H.M. (1974), 'What happened at Hawthorne?' *Science* Vol 18, 4128, pp. 922–32.

Phillips, E.M. and Pugh, D.S. (1998), *How to Get a PhD: A Handbook for Students and their Supervisors* (second edn). Buckingham: Open University Press.

Phillips, R. (1998a), *History Teaching, Nationhood and the State*. London: Cassell.

—— (1998b), 'The politics of history: Some methodological and ethical dilemmas in elite-based research'. *British Educational Research Journal 24*(1), 5–19.

Planter, A. (2006), 'Old school ties', *Lewis*: Granada Television.

Poole, D. (2006, 26 January), 'The real world: David Baddiel, comedian and novelist'. *Independent*.

Poulson, C. (2004, 5 February), 'Don's diary'. *Times Higher Education Supplement*.

Raab, C. (1987), 'Oral history as an instrument of research into Scottish educational policy-making', in G. Moyser and M. Wagstaffe (eds), *Research Methods for Elite Studies*. London: Allen and Unwin.

Russell, L. (2005), 'Teaching the Holocaust in history: Policy and classroom perspectives'. PhD thesis, Goldsmiths College, University of London, London.

Russell, W. (1986), *Educating Rita, Stags and Hens and Blood Brothers*. London: Methuen.

Salon, M. (2007, 1 May), 'Delayed departures', *Afternoon Play*: BBC Radio 4.

Stephen, A. (16 October 2006), 'The truth about the lie detector'. *New Statesman*.

Stoppard, T. (1968), *Rosencrantz and Guildenstern are Dead*. London: Faber and Faber.

Tang, R. and John, S. (1999), 'The "I" in identity: Exploring writer identity in student academic writing through the first person pronoun'. *English for Specific Purposes 18* (Supplement 1), S23–S24.

Teague, C. (2007, 23 June), 'The sound of drums', *Doctor Who* series 3, episode 12: BBC Wales.

Thatcher, M. (1993), *The Downing Street Years*. London: HarperCollins.

Thompson, E.P. (1968), *The Making of the English Working Class*. Harmondsworth: Penguin.

Tosh, J. (1991), *The Pursuit of History*. London: Longman.

Wachowski, L. and Wachowski, A. (1999), *The Matrix*. J. Silver (producer). United States: Warner Bros.

Wakeford, J. (2002, 17 September), 'What goalposts?' *Guardian*.

Weir, P. (1998), *The Truman Show*. E.S. Feldman, S. Rudin, A. Niccol and A. Schroeder (producers). United States: Paramount Pictures.

Wood, V. (1990), *Mens Sana in Thingummy Doodah*. London: Methuen.

Index